WHAT THE BIBLE TEACHES ABOUT
T H E B I B L E

This series of books sets out to present what the Bible actually teaches. We have in mind a readership made up of people of all ages who are comparatively new to the Christian faith or who are feeling their way towards it.

Inevitably, some of the topics considered may be easier to deal with than others. All those who have contributed to the series have in some way or other been involved in a teaching ministry, but in presenting this series of books we are not writing primarily for theological students. Our concern is to help people who are enquiring about the Christian faith and those who have come to believe but who have not had a Christian background. In recent years there has been a tendency to regard Christian doctrine lightly, and to emphasize Christian experience and Christian living. What is needed is a balance between the various aspects of the Christian faith, so that both our experience and our way of life may be measured against the yardstick of what the Bible teaches.

We therefore present this series in the prayerful hope that some seekers after truth may come through to a living faith, and that those whose experience of Christ is new may be built up to become mature men and women of God.

While each book stands on its own feet, we recommend that those who desire to gain a full-orbed picture of what Christianity is all about should study the series as a whole.

EDITOR

WHAT THE BIBLE TEACHES ABOUT

THE
BIBLE

H. D. McDonald

SERIES EDITOR: G. W. KIRBY

Tyndale House Publishers, Inc. Wheaton, Illinois

The following abbreviations are used for versions of the Bible used in this book:
AV/ Authorized (King James) Version; NEB/ New English Bible; RSV/ Revised
Standard Version; Phillips/ The New Testament in Modern English (translated by
J. B. Phillips)

Library of Congress Catalog Card Number 80-80179. ISBN 0-8423-7881-2,
paper. Copyright © 1979 by H. D. McDonald. First published in Great Britain,
under the title *I Want to Know What the Bible Says about the Bible*, by Kingsway
Publications, Ltd. Tyndale House edition published by arrangement with
Kingsway Publications, Ltd. All rights reserved. First Tyndale House printing,
July 1980. Printed in the United States of America.

CONTENTS

'It is the devil's business, father of lies that he is, to persuade you that the Word of God is of no effect, but that it is a vain tale invented by man, and so all that is spoken of Jesus, the Son of God, is but a vain tale.'

From a letter by John Knox to Mrs Bowes, 1553.

'The reason the Son of God appeared was to destroy the works of the devil.'

1 John 3:8

1
GOD'S SELF-DISCLOSURE

The proper place to open up a discussion of what the Bible has to say for itself, and how it would have itself regarded, is to begin where the Bible begins – with God. For God is the whole subject of the Bible. The Bible speaks of God and is where God speaks. God, the living God, is at once the faith and focus of this book. He is the alpha and omega of the biblical word. From first to last the Bible is all about God, about his being, his nature, his character, his purposes, and so forth. The two testaments, the older and the newer, are concerned to disclose these realities about God so that man may attain the ends for which he was created. In such knowledge of God man finds his terrestrial well-being and his eternal good. But such 'knowing' of God can only be because of God's willingness to be known. God's 'know-ingness' is, therefore, one and the same thing with his revealing. For only in the Bible is the living God revealed. 'He is known through revelation alone. This Lord God is the God of the biblical revelation.'[1]

Revelation

We often speak of the Christian revelation or the biblical revelation, and in so doing tacitly equate Christian faith with biblical faith. And rightly so, for Christianity claims to have a distinctive revelation of God which is contained within its scriptures. This distinctive Christian revelation is founded upon God's earlier self-disclosure to the people of Israel, but for his ultimate unveiling we are carried on into the New Testament, so that we have to affirm with Søren Kierkegaard that 'The New

Testament settles what Christianity is.'[2] The concept of revelation is, therefore, primary in our discussion: here is our starting-point.

Now the subject of revelation has become central in contemporary debate. And the ensuing controversy goes to the very heart of the Christian claim and concerns the very nature of the gospel itself. Some modern writers have even called in question the whole idea of a divine revelation. F. Gerald Dowling, for example, gave his book the question-begging title, *Has Christianity a Revelation?*[3] He doubts that it has and considers that the sparsity of words in the Bible for 'to reveal' is a sufficient justification for its denial. But the validity of such concordance mustering of a term cannot be taken in itself as conclusive.

It is, of course, true that all religions lay claim to their 'revelations', in the sense, at any rate, of their possessing some indications of a divine 'somewhat' behind the world of appearances. But such 'revelations', common to these religions, are 'accidentals' because they are not grounded in historical factualities. Christian faith, by contrast, proclaims itself to be not just 'a' but 'the' one authentic self-disclosure of God in the decisive sense of its being 'once for all', and consequently unique and final. Or, stating the fact as we have put it elsewhere,

> The idea of God *making himself known* in acts of redemption and judgement and in prophetic, interpretative utterances pervades the Bible. It is not so much *a* biblical idea, as it is *the* biblical idea.[4]

The term 'revelation' has become especially associated with one book of the Bible, the *Revelation* of St John the Divine. But in truth all the sixty-six books have equal right to the designation. For these several writings constitute the one self-disclosure of God in his triunity of Father, Son and Holy Spirit. Apart from this revelation we would hardly know *that* God is, and know precious little of *what* he is.

But what precisely do we mean by revelation? To answer this question we must consider *the idea of revelation*.

The word 'revelation', so fundamental to our Christian faith, has but few references in the Bible itself. It does not occur at all in the Old Testament, although the verbal form 'to reveal' or 'to be revealed' is found several times in Daniel and Isaiah. The noun appears a dozen times in the New Testament where it is used to translate the Greek word *apokalupsis*. In none of these references, however, does it connote quite what is intended when we speak of the Christian revelation or the biblical revelation. Too much play must not, however, be made of these twin facts. To declare, as Dowling does, that the idea of a revelation of God is not, for these reasons, a characteristic biblical idea is altogether false. Revelation, admittedly, is no more a characteristic biblical word than many other of our necessary theological terms. But it does not follow that the idea of revelation does not convey an essential biblical note. So omnipresent is the thought of God making himself known, of disclosing his presence, of making manifest truths about himself previously concealed and otherwise undiscoverable, that the conviction is inescapable that God cannot be known at all by man unless and until he makes himself known.

It is in truth these very terms, 'making known', 'making manifest', and the like, which the Bible uses with more or less heightened significance to bring out the thought of God's supernatural self-disclosure. We must therefore affirm with Leon Morris that

> if we wish to know what the writers of the biblical books thought about revelation we must take into account a good deal more than the passages which contain the noun 'revelation' and the verb 'reveal'.[5]

Dewey M. Beegle, as Morris notes, collects a host of terms which he considers convey without doubt the idea of a divine unveiling.[6]

In the King James Version of the Bible the verb 'to reveal' occurs some fifty times, of which twenty-three come in the Old Testament to translate the Hebrew word *gelah*, or its Aramaic equivalent *g'lah*. The root meaning of this term is 'nakedness'. When applied to revelation it suggests the uncovering of an object to perception or the removal of an obstacle so that what would be otherwise obscured is openly unveiled.

The English word 'revelation', which derives from the Latin, conveys the thought of the drawing back of a veil, the disclosure of something which would otherwise remain hidden. The term is, therefore, almost an exact equivalent for the idea of 'uncovering', and thus carries the thought of a 'showing forth' or 'laying bare' of what was previously hidden. In some such way are we to understand God's disclosure of himself. Basically, to reveal is to communicate. God's revelation is, therefore, *God communicating.*

Yet the idea of revelation is not something altogether foreign to us, something unparalleled in our normal life's experiences. There is a sense in which all reality is self-communicative.[7] Nothing can be known unless some facts and features reveal its presence. This is true even in inanimate things. But the more we ascend in the scale of being, and the more personal beings become, the more disclosure becomes necessary and possible. Where individuality exists with its powers of feeling and volition, there exist too the actualities of communication. It follows that all things must, in their measure, disclose themselves if they are to be known and understood at all. With inanimate phenomena there can, of course, be no willing giving forth or holding back. Where, however, the human mind and spirit are concerned, self-revelation is a *sine qua non* of knowledge. Until there is this self-disclosure we are shut off from real contact and communication. Where there is no readiness to disclose himself an individual remains isolated in island aloofness, beyond the reach of the other. Communication is essential for communion. 'In some such way the other has to speak, else he remains an impenetrable mystery if indeed he can be recognized as personal at all.'[8]

Because man is a personal being he can enter into relationships. But this presupposes the power of utterance, the possibility of giving a direct revelation of one's innermost selfhood. In a world where friendships are a real experience the possibility of giving personal communication from mind to mind is no strange affair. We are all aware of that 'overagainstness' in relation to 'the other', and how we can only enter into an understanding fellowship with those who admit us into their inner life. The knowledge that is most necessary for us to know is that of self-disclosure. Our own experience testifies that, between individuals capable of it, direct revelation is a constant fact.

The media of this communication are mainly speech and act. It is by these that a personal disclosure is the most surely made. So with God. He reveals himself in speech and act. And there are numerous references in scripture to God speaking and God acting. With God, however, the two seem to coalesce: for him to speak is to act, and to act is to speak. And it is just because God has spoken and acted in revelation that man can respond in faith. For faith is precisely the response of the individual in the totality of his being to God's self-disclosure. God is more than a mere idea. He is a personal, spiritual reality, and, as such, he can communicate himself in a personal way to man. Since God is a Selfhood, an Ego, he must proclaim himself to man if man is to know him at all. He must, as Brunner says, 'name his name to us'. For the name that we give him on our own account is not *his* name.

The names of God

For a full appreciation of revelation, therefore, due regard must be given to the many names of God which appear in the biblical record; in naming himself, God is at the same time disclosing his nature. Essentially in scripture, as J. A. Motyer observes, the name stands for the 'person revealed' and 'the person actively present.'[9] Motyer notes that where God's name is implicated he is personally involved. God's name is associated throughout the Old Testament, and specifically in the Psalms, with attributes in which he displays himself, in his righteousness, faithfulness, holiness, salvation, mercy, and the like. And people are said to react towards the Name in such a way as to indicate that it expresses the quality of God as revealed. His name can, for example, be blasphemed (Isaiah 52:5), polluted (Jeremiah 34:16), and so forth. On the other hand, it can be loved (Psalm 5:11), be praised (Joel 2:26), be thought upon (Malachi 3:16), be waited on (Psalm 52:9). The peoples who have not reckoned with

God's disclosure of his name 'each walk in the name of its god', but, declares Micah the prophet, 'we will walk in the name of the Lord our God' (Micah 4:5).

In the Bible, then, the names of God, as Louis Berkhof declares, 'are not of human invention, but of divine origin. ... They are given by God himself with assurance that they contain in a certain measure a revelation of the Divine Being.'[10] Left to himself, even the most sophisticated of men can only proffer notions of God which are pale and paltry. They speak about the Ground of Being, Ultimate Reality, the Unknown Somewhat, the Final Factor of existence, the Cohesive Force of the universe, and such like, which neither evoke response nor inspire worship. As Bavinck remarks, left to ourselves, 'We would deny every one of his attributes.'[11] Everywhere men who either do not know or who have rejected the biblical revelation protest against those attributes which God in his self-disclosure has especially associated with his name, his love, his righteousness, his justice, his sovereignty, and so forth. Yet it is 'God himself who revealed all his excellency and puts his names upon our lips.'[12] God alone can name himself and can speak of himself. And only 'because God has revealed himself in his name we can now designate Him by that name in various forms.'[13]

Our subject does not call for a discussion of these various names for God. That has indeed been fittingly done by others. We may note, however, that the names of God were revealed progressively and in the historical context in which they could best be understood.

> The truly remarkable factors in the disclosure of God's names are these, that the living God transcendently and absolutely discloses his name in historical revelation, and that the successively revealed names of God signal distinctive epochs in the progressive manifestation of God's redemptive purpose.[14]

As Brunner affirms, 'through God only can God be known.'[15] All knowledge of God must then start with the assurance of God's willingness to reveal himself; and ground itself on the certainty that he has. Thus is revelation, as Carl Henry has it, 'a divinely initiated activity, God's free communication by which alone he turns his personal privacy into a deliberate disclosure of his reality.'[16]

Knowing God, therefore, is a matter of God's self-revealing, not of man's own discovery; for that would make it a subject of mere human originating. It is an error to conceive of revelation as resulting from some men's unique power of insight. Schleiermacher was responsible for the popular, but false, notion that the bearers of revelation were religious geniuses who because of their profounder sympathies were able, in a greater measure than the common run of men, to penetrate deeper into the ultimate secret of the world's unity. As seers, these rare spirits caught the final spirituality of existence. And what they discovered they sought to make known – haltingly – for there were things they 'felt' which defied explanation. But revelation is not genius touched by emotion. Especially is it not something merely parasitic on the insights of others. Revelation properly understood is God's doing; it is the making known of that which no man 'on his own' could ever discover. It is the divine unfolding of the *musterion tou theou* – the mystery of God. It is the self-disclosure of God, of his being, his purpose and his grace. Revelation is consequently a corollary of Christian theism; and the absence of revelation is quite unthinkable. Revelation is the basic and acknowledged fact of the Christian faith. There may be 'religion without revelation'; but it is certainly not the Christian religion. 'If God is personal and if he is personally related to us, it is fitting that he should wish to reveal himself to us by special means . . . the particularity of Judaeo-Christian revelation is undoubtedly a "scandal" to those who think of God as an impersonal Absolute; but it is wholly reasonable to those who think of him as the person in whose image every human person is created.'[17]

The stages of revelation

The distinctions between general and special revelation; and natural and supernatural revelation, bring into relief two stages or aspects of God's unveiling which it is important to keep in

mind. There is a general revelation of God which God makes
continually to all men; and there is his special revelation which
he has made known through his chosen people and which
reaches its culmination in Christ. General revelation we may say
comes to man as man; special revelation to the same man as a
sinner. But as a sinner man has not ceased to be man. He has
rather added to himself new needs which require additional
provisions that he might fulfil the ends for which he was created.
Thus is God's special self-disclosure addressed to man in his sin,
guilt and helplessness. In Psalm 19, these two ideas of revelation
are brought together. The Psalm begins with praise to the glory
of God, who, as Creator, has written his signature on the spacious
firmament. And it ends with praise for the mercy of God, the
God of the covenant, who has visited man with his saving word.
It is on the reality of this higher revelation that the psalmist bases
his prayer for salvation from sin which ends with the acclamation
of an adoring heart, 'O Lord, my rock and my redeemer.'

The distinction suggested between the other alternatives,
natural and supernatural revelation, is also useful. Natural
revelation is communicated through natural phenomena,
whereas supernatural revelation puts the stress on a direct in-
tervention of God into the natural order. It has the aspect, as
Brunner says, of 'an incursion from another dimension'.
Revelation as natural is addressed to men generally as intelligent
beings, and is for that reason, at least ideally, accessible to all.
Supernatural special revelation is, by contrast, essentially
soteriological; it is, that is to say, concerned with man's salvation.
It is, therefore, addressed to man as sinner, that in and by the
knowledge of God's redeeming grace he might come to enjoy
restored fellowship with him. Natural revelation, therefore,
assures to man as God's creature a possible knowledge of himself
as Moral Ruler of the universe. Supernatural revelation comes as
God's forgiving love to the same creature as sinfully guilty before
him.

Natural revelation is, then, in this sense, as H. R. Mackintosh
says, 'primary', with its threefold constituents of nature, the
human conscience, and history. And so do they provide all the
conditions for the rise and progress of true faith in the human

spirit. For however true it is that man's nature has been changed through sin this 'primary' revelation remains as a witness to man of what he has become. 'God's general revelation is presupposed not only because the revelation of scripture declares it to be the basis of man's moral and spiritual responsibility to God. In an even deeper sense it is mankind's revolt against this general revelation, both in Adam and on each one's individual count, that constitutes human beings sinners. The universal revelation in creation makes all humans responsible and frames their guilt.'[18]

John Calvin recognized this reality of God's general revelation. 'On each of his works', he declares, God's 'glory is engraven in characters so bright, so distinct, and so illustrious, that none, however dull and illiterate can plead ignorance as an excuse'.[19] But, as Calvin saw clearly, 'by sin man perverts into idolatry that which God has given him.'[20] The result is that man everywhere has failed to note the heavenly hallmark upon the universe. The light of nature, the works of God in creation and providence, may render man inexcusable; but still, as the Westminster Catechism declares, 'they are not sufficient to give that knowledge of God and his will, which is necessary to salvation.' This means that in Christian eyes, general and natural revelation are at best an indirect form of revelation, although a presupposition of the special and supernatural revelation of the Christian faith. Even the prophets of ancient times declared that God is Lord of total reality. Nevertheless they were aware how baffling was the speech of God in the created universe and human history. They knew, as Pascal says, that God's reality is not so clearly seen in the natural order that its certainty is inevitable; nor yet are disorder and disarray so obtrusive as to make atheism final. It was in the light of God's disclosure as Israel's Redeemer that the prophets found a new significance in the events of history, the behaviour of nature, and the experiences of life.

Thus while the two modes of revelation are distinguished, the Bible itself insists upon their permanent relationship and interconnection. They belong together, each somehow incomplete without the other. Revelation in its most general sense is rooted in creation and in those relations with his intelligent creatures into which God has brought himself by giving them existence. God's purpose was to create a fellowship of men with whom he could have communion. By the entrance of sin and the destruction of this fellowship, the 'natural' relationship was disrupted and the knowledge of God blurred. He therefore initiated a new mode of revelation conditioned upon the new needs of men.

The introduction of special revelation must not, however, be regarded as a makeshift measure. Sin did not take God by surprise. The course of history was not something either unforeseen or uncontrollable by God. Consequently revelation in its dual aspect was God's intended revelation from the beginning, its single purpose to realize the ends of creation. It is then by means of special revelation that the truths given in general revelation are illuminated and vindicated. 'It is not nature that opens the door to God,' says Helmut Thielicke, 'it's the other way around: God opens the door to nature.'[21] What is Braille to a blind man is God's clear signature 'writ large' to one whose eyes have been opened. To the natural man the reality of general revelation may profit little, but from the vantage point of special revelation the full speech of general revelation is heard. In the end the biblical message is not 'Listen to nature!', 'Look to history!' or even, 'Follow conscience!' Rather is it, 'Hear God!', 'See the Eternal!', 'Follow the Lord!'.

The modes of revelation

In contrast with general revelation, the revelation of God to which the Bible points is *special*, that is, directed towards a specified end. It is 'saving' in its purpose. Not that the revelation of which the Bible speaks is somehow divorced from nature or history. This cannot be. In the biblical account God is not set apart from his world in deistic fashion. Indeed, the great prophets were foremost in proclaiming God as the Lord both of nature and of history. And throughout the whole Bible, in the New Testament no less than in the Old, both nature and history are regarded as the single theatre of God's saving action on man's behalf. Both serve his one sovereign purpose. Passages in the Old Testament, like the creation, the Flood, the crossing of the Red Sea, are standing reminders of the relation between historic events and the God of nature. For 'the conception of a God who works in history is inseparably linked to his manifestation in natural phenomena. He is what Nature, as well as history, reveals himself to be.'[22] In the New Testament the life and ministry of Jesus show clearly and repeatedly a coordination between historic and natural happenings in which God actively works out his purposes. Throughout the biblical account, then, there is the intertwining of the natural and the historical in God's progressive self-disclosure. This observation has significance for the way God reveals himself, for such a revelation will not preclude, but will rather involve the media of natural phenomena and historical events.

God's revelation will accordingly be a gradual disclosure of himself in ways appropriate to its time: the way, indeed, the Bible presents it. It came 'in many and various ways', in 'bits and pieces' (Hebrews 1:1). Sometimes through a dream or symbol; sometimes by God's mighty acts of natural disaster or deliverance; sometimes by priestly ceremony or by prophetic word, until in the 'fulness of time' God's final self-disclosure was accomplished (cf. Galatians 4:4; Hebrews 1:1f., etc.).

Generally in the patriarchal age the media of revelation were external; in the prophetic period they were internal. Where the former age knew symbols and theophanies, the latter saw the prophets under the instant constraints of God's Spirit in their hearts (cf. e.g. Isaiah 58:19; Ezekiel 2:2; Micah 3:8; cf. 1 Peter 1:11).

This broad distinction cannot, however, be taken as absolute. That earlier age was by no means restricted to external media for God's self-disclosure. God's chosen men of those days had their dreams and visions, but usually without specific reference to their divine source (cf. Genesis 37:5f.; 40:5f.; 41:7f. but see Genesis 20:3, 6; 31:11, 24, etc.). In the prophetic period, likewise, God is still said to make himself known 'in a dream' (cf. e.g. Daniel 7:1). Even in New Testament days God continued this medium of disclosing the purpose of his saving revelation in the form of divinely induced dreams (cf. Matthew 1:20; 2:12, 13, 19, 22; cf. Matthew 27:19). Visions too had their place in the prophetic period (cf. e.g. Daniel 2:19; Ezekiel 11:24) and these were continued also into the New Testament as a specified method by which God disclosed his purpose (cf. Acts 9:10, 12; 10:17, 19; 11:5; 16:9, 10; 18:9; cf. Acts 26:19; 2 Corinthians 12:1).

But the prophets were withal men who spake from God and for him, God's spokesmen (cf. 1 Samuel 28:6; 2 Samuel 24:11; 2 Kings 21:10; 2 Chronicles 20:20; 36:12, 16, etc.). From God these chosen men received their word. In his name they gave it. But whatever the mode of God's self-disclosure, one fundamental fact remained constant: the spiritual quality of the revelation was not derived ultimately from the chosen organ but from the One whose purpose it was to make himself known. In whatever diversity of form and at whatever stage it was given, it is always the revelation of the same God.[23] It is therefore proper to insist that

> no one has private licence to exalt any of these varieties of divine revelation above another, or to dichotomize God's disclosure, or to isolate one strand from the others.[24]

In the Old Testament, however, Moses stands out as the dominant figure in the process of God's revelation, and with him 'the Lord used to speak face to face, as a man speaks with his friend' (Exodus 33:11). He was, it appears, admitted into a relationship with God not accorded to others. But not on that account is it said that the revelations given to him are superior to other modes of revelation. Even the revelation through the medium of dreams is not considered less fitting; for throughout the whole biblical account, importance is placed on *what* is revealed rather than on *how*; on the divine Subject of the revelation rather than the specific organ of its communication.

With Moses, however, revelation entered on a new mode or stage. For the patriarchs, God's self-disclosings were occasional and circumstantial, given in the nature of separate events and specifically related to some divine command to be fulfilled. Such revelations belonged to a decisive moment and mood in their lives, rather than to the whole course of their activity.

In the case of Moses, on the other hand, revelation became more sustained in character, more didactic in style. The four books following Genesis are dominated by his person, while the giving of the first law and the second, on the basis of God's own manifestation of himself, takes up a large place in these writings. In Moses God's revelation, with the demands made upon his chosen people, is now mediated through a human instrument who became the inspired organ of the divine unveiling. Old Testament revelation appears here to have reached its highest point through personal fellowship with God. Close as was the communion between God and Abraham his 'friend' (cf. 2 Chronicles 2:7; Isaiah 41:8; cf. James 2:23), the 'face to face', or as it is literally, 'mouth to mouth' relation Moses enjoyed with God was even closer and more intimate; so that the divine epitaph could sum it up: 'And there has not arisen a prophet since in Israel like Moses, whom the Lord knew face to face.' (Deuteronomy 34:10.)

The word 'prophet' in this passage puts us on the right track for an understanding of the distinctive feature of God's revelation. It is to the sustained character of the Mosaic revelation, combined with the mode of its communication through a personal medium, that we apply the term 'prophetic'. Moses was himself aware of the special character of his own position as an intermediary between God and man in the remarkable declaration of Deuteronomy 18:15–22, where he speaks of the coming great prophet who will, like himself, speak in God's name the words God has put in his mouth. And that coming great prophet we know in the light of fulfilment in Christ to have had in fact a more 'face to face' relation with God as one knowing God and speaking for God (cf. John 1:1f.; Matthew 11:25–27, etc.) than possibly even Moses could have envisaged.

But whatever in the Old Testament was the chosen mode of God's self-disclosure, its supernatural character was nowhere compromised. Whatever was the selected medium of the revelation, whether it was by lot, dream, vision, theophany, institution, or prophecy, the one fact remains constant: it is God, the living personal God, who is communicating himself to man. Revelation is from God and is for man: God is the source of it, and man the object of it.

Thus at its highest point revelation moves in the realm of personal relationships. As personality is the essential nature of man, it is just here that God has disclosed himself in his clearest and final form – 'in Face like my face' as Browning puts it (cf. 2 Corinthians 4:6; cf. Matthew 17:2; Genesis 32:30; 1 Corinthians 16:11; Psalm 105:4; 119:135, etc.).

Thus the Christian revelation focuses upon the living personality of Christ as the final exegete of God. Here is God's last self-disclosure in divine deed and word expressed in terms of an actual human life. 'Incarnation is the highest possible form of divine revelation to us since human personality is the highest created form of existence known to us.'[25]

The fullness of time had come in the fifteenth year of Tiberius Caesar when Pontius Pilate was governor of Judaea. God at last spoke in One who is Son of God – then was the life manifested. Then God appeared in the arena of human history and experience. The Word was made flesh. The Truth of God was embodied in a life. The literature of heaven was translated into the language of earth. Hitherto in nature and in history God had revealed his purpose. Now in Christ he made bare his heart in a final unfolding of himself for which he had long prepared by the selecting and shaping of the people of Israel. Thus is the record of the Old Testament a prelude of the New: the Old is the promise, the New the fulfilment. They belong together, and both together constitute 'the history of our salvation' in its prefiguration and its performance, in its intimation and its realization. The history of the Old Testament in which great personalities played so vital a part, and the personality of Jesus Christ in the New Testament which is decisively grounded in history, together set forth that special self-disclosure of God in the knowledge of which man can fulfil his 'chief end' as redeemed and restored by divine grace. This is the motive, the movement, and the meaning of the whole drama which leads to the cross on the green hill. Here God's 'saving' revelation is brought to completion. 'Jesus Christ is', then, as Tom Torrance declares, 'the place where God has made room for himself in the midst of our human existence as the place where man on earth and in history may meet and have communion with the heavenly Father.'[26]

We may say, then, that the highest and most perfect form of God's revelation in the Old Testament focuses on the historic figure of Moses; and in the New Testament on the historical reality of Jesus Christ. Moses was the centre of that which prefigured the true; and Christ the centre of the true itself. Moses was central in the fleeting, Christ is central in the final. These are the two foci of the ellipse of revelation: 'For the law was given through Moses; grace and truth came through Jesus Christ.' (John 1:17.)

2
THE BIBLICAL REVELATION

The first chapter discussed revelation as the basic presupposition of our Christian faith since, as Bavinck says, it is 'with the reality of revelation Christianity stands or falls.'[1] Revelation gives us a map of the spiritual world. Or, more significantly, as Bernard Ramm puts it, revelation is the autobiography of God, the story in which God narrates himself.[2] In divine revelation God disclosed *himself*. It provides a knowledge *about* God which is *from* God and which, in the apprehension of faith, brings man to a knowledge *of* God.

The Bible, then, is God's own autobiography. Now, an autobiography differs from a biography. A biography is written by another, by someone who cannot, in the nature of the case, penetrate to the ultimate intentions, motives, desires, and so forth, of the subject of his research. But an autobiography is different. In it the writer professes to tell the truth about himself, to give the reader a glimpse of his inner soul. It is, however, doubtful whether there is such a production as an altogether honest human autobiography. No man does really succeed in painting himself 'warts and all', if for no other reason than that no man has been able to master the ancient Greek dictum to know himself. But it is otherwise with God. God's revelation is his disclosure of himself in his relationship with man, and, as such, is perfect and sufficient for that end.

By saying that God discloses himself we are not suggesting that in his revelation he has, so to speak, exhausted himself. He has given himself in his fullness to man, but not the fullness of himself. Those who repudiate the whole concept of revelation sometimes object that to allow the reality of a divine self-disclosure would rob God of mystery. But the contention is not really serious. Even in God's clearest disclosure there is in some sense an aspect of concealment, an awareness that what we know, we know imperfectly (cf. 1 Corinthians 13:9). Luther constantly referred to the 'hidden' God behind the God 'revealed'. In this distinction he was merely drawing out what the Bible itself so often indicates, namely, that God remains forever beyond what man has been given to know of him. 'His understanding is unsearchable' (Isaiah 40:28). He is at the same time the God who works wonders, who has manifested his might among the peoples (Psalm 77:14), yet he is the God who hides himself (Isaiah 45:15).

God in his revelation – God 'for us' – we know, for that he has revealed. But God 'for himself' we do not know, for that he has not disclosed. He has revealed such knowledge about himself as relates to man's salvation: his triunity, his sovereignty, his faithfulness, his love, his grace, and the like. But there is mystery remaining, a mystery of God's being that we may never know, not even, perhaps, when we meet him 'face to face'. 'Even in his revelation God does not cease to be clothed in mystery; his revelation never exhausts the mysterious fulness of his nature.'[3] God is then greater than what he has disclosed himself to be. He 'transcends his own revelation. We do not have exhaustive knowledge of the self-revealing God, but what we do know about divine things is determined by his disclosure.'[4] But what we know is enough for us to know. 'The secret things belong to the Lord our God; but the things that are revealed belong to us and to our children for ever' (Deuteronomy 29:29). That is surely the sum of the matter as it concerns the question of revelation and mystery.

Earlier pages have indicated in a general way some features of God's self-disclosure. It is both personal and progressive. God revealed himself to man as man was in a position to receive such knowledge. We must, however, add a passing reference to other features of God's self-disclosure before going on to indicate the relationship between God's past revelation and the scriptures we now possess.

The uniqueness of the biblical revelation

First of all we must insist that the Christian revelation is unique. Precisely by this claim is it distinguished from all other religions. While these do speak of a 'revelation' of the object of their reverence, the vital issue turns on the nature of the 'revelation' they claim. Such religions, whether of the mystical or speculative type, differ radically in character and content from the absolute revelation of the Christian gospel. The incidental theophanies of the mystical type are at bottom merely an expression of a general revelation, of a claimed union with the 'ultimate ground of being' within the depths of the human soul.

The speculative types, who assert that 'the essence of religion' is expressed in many varieties, are equally opposed to the Christian proclamation of a revelation, unique, final, and unrepeatable. In such views revelation does not really take place at all, since all nature, history, and human existence are alike the unfolding of the one 'divine' life. There is no place here for a special self-disclosure of God as a personal and distinct being. But Christianity has, and knows itself to have, a unique revelation of God.

The historical nature of revelation

Second, the Christian revelation is historical. Here is a subject that requires a volume on its own. But we must realize that God's revelation is truly historically founded. God's self-disclosures recorded in the Old Testament are linked with actual historical events, of which the crossing of the Red Sea may be taken as an example. And the New Testament gospel is likewise factually dated (cf. e.g. Luke 1:5; 2:1, 2). It almost seems trite, therefore, to say that if God is to reveal himself at all it cannot be apart from history. The story of God's historical unveiling is in fact the content of the biblical record. God's revelation is thus securely based in historical actualities.

And the history of which we speak is, of course, true, matter-of-fact history. Biblical history is not some strange, airy sort of meta-history, as the Barthian school teaches. The so-called *Heilsgeschichte* – 'holy history' – school would relegate God's revelatory acts to a ghetto-like realm hovering above and beyond 'the accidents of history'. Yet however much it may be stressed that biblical history is 'sacred history' it is still actual and factual history. In seeking to prise the Christian message from its sure anchorage in sheer historical situations, Bultmann resolved faith into a sort of churchly musing on an unknowable figure of the past. Pannenberg would simply identify revelation with total history, but this thesis undercuts the uniqueness of the biblical revelation by allowing that there are other ways to God. If all history is equally revelatory, there is no special history, – and if there is no absolute claim for the Christian revelation, there is no 'scandal of particularity'.

But God must neither be excluded from all history nor restricted to some special type of history. Carl Henry's seventh thesis puts the matter in right perspective:

> God reveals himself not only universally in the history of the cosmos and of the nations, but also redemptively within this external history (of Israel) in unique saving acts.[5]

The Bible itself certainly directs attention to God's activities in the history of nations beyond Israel. Prophet after prophet uttered divine predictions against them. Daniel's life for God was in great measure bound up with God's dealings with Babylon. Cyrus, king of Persia, is declared to be God's 'anointed', his 'shepherd', to fulfil his purposes (cf. Isaiah 44:28; 45:1). And many nations are brought into the sweep of the prophetic word to fulfil in their way and time God's grand design. Yet with Israel God has a specific relationship, for God was active in her history in a way not evident in that of other nations. All God's treatment of Israel points to the uniqueness of his acts in her history as the medium of his special self-disclosure. Considered merely from the historical standpoint the history of the Jewish people is tied to universal history by the thread of analogy. Nevertheless, it has a uniqueness as the specific sphere of God's revelatory acts. Yet this 'distinctiveness of Israel's history is not in anything Israel has done'.[6] It is based altogether on God's electing love. That is the paradox to which the whole scripture testifies. There is an exclusiveness in God's love; it is a love which 'chose' Israel as its 'elected' object for his purpose of self-revelation. 'Either we must accept this idea of choice on the part of God with its necessary accompaniment of exclusiveness, or we have to hold to a doctrine of the love of God other than that which is biblical.'[7]

The history, then, in which God discloses himself is history in the sense of being concrete actualities and events within the context of world history. But it is *divine* history – *sacred* history – in the sense that here God has acted specifically with a view to man's salvation.

Yet this disclosure of God in biblical history is not just a series of 'naked acts'. Rather were they made known specifically as God's acts and divinely interpreted in the light of his saving purpose. A bare historical incident as such is not a divine revelation, any more than a divine revelation can be given apart from historical events. Some scholars advocate that the biblical seers and prophets and, indeed, the apostolic preachers, looked at certain events either real or alleged and, so to speak, read God into them. But for God's acts to be revelatory not only the historical actualities but the meaning of such events also must be divinely disclosed. And the meaning and the interpretation must be inherent in the act-event, not imposed upon it by some religious seer. God must in fact interpret his own actions, disclose to his spokesmen their revelatory significance. 'Deeds by themselves', declares Leon Morris, 'are not revelation.'[8] God did not just perform a series of acts and leave it to those who were able, to detect them as his working. This is no divine charade, as some suppose, to be solved by the God-inspired guesswork of human spectators, but something that commends itself as true. Take any single event of the biblical record: those who witness its happening did not for the most part understand it as a divine self-disclosure. They were like those watching in our day a television drama with the sound cut off. Aware of something going on, they could not make sense out of the successive happenings. 'For revelation to be discerned the right interpretation is needed.'[9] The words are necessary to the meaning. And such meaning is born of the wisdom which is from above.

So, then, we insist most strongly that without the acts there would be no revelation, yet these acts could never be read as revelatory without the disclosure of their divine significance. Christianity is indeed rooted in history; it is based four-square on events and facts. But unexplained activity is not revelation. The capricious goings-on of the heathen godlings who act impetuously and devastatingly leave it to their devotees to guess at their whims and desires. But in biblical faith it is not so.

Facts, and their God-given meaning, alone equal revelation. Events plus explanation – this is the pattern of the whole biblical record. At some points, indeed, as in the case of prophetic declarations of coming events, the divine explanation may precede the divine acts. But this merely underscores the importance of the historical occurrence for the divine self-disclosure. And it shows that the biblical writers by no means sat lightly to history. Their aim was, under God, to bring out of all history specific historical events and to specify his intention of self-disclosure in bringing them to pass. This insistence carries with it the fact that the history must be taken as true in the sequence of events as they are recorded. If Israel's history took place otherwise than the biblical account sets it down, then surely the interpretation must also be otherwise. 'It must in some way be the whole complex of events together with their interpretation which constitute the revelation of God in history.'[10] Reconstruction implies re-interpretation. If the interpretation is to be taken as valid so also must the history be regarded as authentic. If the facts are re-shuffled, then their valuation is ruined.

What is true of the Old Testament history is true of the New Testament story. Here are facts about Christ and their interpretation, their collocation and their valuation. Some have sought to deny the facts, for example that of the virgin birth, and yet keep the valuation. Others have sought to deny the interpretation the New Testament puts upon the facts. But the facts and values go together. The revelation in Christ is full and final only when it is seen, not in this act or that word, but in every deed and word, and in the divinely communicated interpretation and application of every deed and word, that is, in the whole Christ of the whole New Testament. The Bible then presents a book of God-given facts and God-inspired valuations.

The propositional nature of revelation

The meaning of the events is then communicated by God and, of course, necessarily in words. This means that there is a propositional aspect in revelation. In the present anti-intellectualistic mood it is the fashion to deny that the Bible sets forth statements on divine truth. Typical of a large force of contemporary theological opinion, William Temple boldly declared that there is no such thing as revealed truth. Temple was admittedly concerned to emphasize that in revelation God meets man personally and intimately.[11] But the question arises, How could we be sure that it is God we are meeting if he has not told us so? How could we know the sort of God he is unless he made himself known in specific actions which are shown to be his? The contention therefore, as Hugo Meynell says,

> that revelation is primarily of a person, and not of propositions, is not to the point; since *that* God is revealed as a person, and *what* kind of person it is that God is revealed to be, and *how* he is so revealed, can be expressed only in propositions.[12]

It must then be asserted that

> the Bible is throughout based upon the belief that God has unveiled to men something of his own character and will, and that he has spoken through men, in whose mouth he has put his words.[13]

It is right to insist that it is God himself we would know, not just a set of truths about him which, James Orr agrees, would be a mere 'doctrinaire' view of revelation. It is certainly God we need – the very God himself. This need of man, on the one hand, and the character of the biblical record on the other, suggest that the dichotomy between the idea of revelation as propositional and as personal must somehow be false. Christian faith is certainly not belief in a set of propositions, not yet is it what Barth and others contend, belief apart from propositions. 'There is more in faith than assent to propositions; but to allow that there is more is not to disallow that assent to propositions has its place in faith.'[14] Saving faith is, rather, as we have insisted in another place, mediated *through* propositions.[15] Revelation as the Bible presents it comes as both Spirit and Truth. It is in the union of Logos and Dynamis that its essential nature lies. Through what it declares *of* God, it conducts us to a knowledge of *God himself.*

God's revelation, then, in act and word is the first and fundamental fact. The divine self-disclosure came immediately either by some chosen media, or through chosen men of God to those who first received the revelation. In the light of the particular disclosure, the people of the time were called upon to make the appropriate response, to trust its promises, heed its warnings, follow its commands, or whatever. But a day came when those who heralded the divine acts or were given their revelatory meaning, passed from the scene, and the habits of men changed. For the people of the time, God's unveiling was the decisive thing. But revelation would have been still-born and limited were it not in some way made available for the coming generations. 'An oral communication given to a man of God, to one generation or to a chosen people, is not sufficient. It is indispensable that the message be put into writing.'[16]

The written word

For this reason God in his wisdom chose to commit to writing the account of his acts and the form of his words. In no other way, it would seem, could it be better perpetuated. As John Calvin says,

> Since no daily responses are given from heaven, and the Scriptures are the only records in which God has been pleased to consign his truth to perpetual remembrance, the full authority which they ought to possess with the faithful is not recognized, unless they are believed to have come from heaven, as directly as if God had been heard giving utterance to them.[17]

In the written record, then, man is brought into contact with

God's unfolding revelation in every era, and thus made contemporary with the divine unveiling which finds its culmination in Christ the Lord. So does God's revelation confront each age directly, immediately, and personally.

Here two notable facts emerge. The first, and most obvious, is that scripture is a record of revelation. Clearly the revelation was prior to the record. Men of God were commanded to write or claim to have written of what they had seen of God's act or heard of God's words (cf. Exodus 17:14; Numbers 5:23; Joshua 8:32; 26:26; 2 Chronicles 26:22; Jeremiah 30:2; Habakkuk 2:2; Revelation 1:11, 19, etc.). Only a revelation so embodied can be secure; only in this way could its original form be preserved in its purity and distinctiveness. If there were no adequate record, each new generation would need again the revelation. Bethlehem and Calvary would have to be repeated to bring God to man. But having the record it becomes for the ages following the original revelation the vehicle of objective truth about him of whom the disclosure was made.

In the Bible, therefore, we have a record of God's unveiling in dreams, in visions, in theophanies, in the utterances of prophets, in God's own spoken words, and so forth. Also set down are the reactions of people in thought and life to what God has disclosed of himself, as well as the reactions of those to whom the disclosure was made. It must then be evident that the record is necessary, if the revelation is to be preserved. God's revelation would not be available and guaranteed to people of later ages unless it found an adequate medium of transmission. The fact that we possess the Bible is evidence that God willed to secure his revelation in written record. 'Either,' says P. T. Forsyth, 'by a continuous Apostolate supernaturally secured in the *Charisma veritatis*, as Rome claims, or by a book which should be the real successor of the Apostles, with a real authority on the vital matters of truth and faith. But we discard the supernatural pope for the supernatural book.'[18] It is in the book, the Bible, by means of written language, that God's revelation finds permanent form and so is given immediacy, catholicity and durability. What we have said so far can, then, be summed up in the words of James Orr:

The proposition may be laid down that, if a revelation has been given, it is natural and reasonable to expect that a record will be made or kept of the stages of that revelation, either by its immediate recipients, or by those who stand within the circle of the revelation, and are possessed in an eminent degree of its Spirit.[19]

But this consideration leads on to our second point, that in the scriptures revelation and record coalesce. While both differ in idea, here they dovetail. The Bible *is* God's book, the book of the divine revelation. Consequently 'it is only in the measure that we can trust the record that we can apprehend the revelation. If we cannot believe the record we cannot recover the acts of God or the inspired thinking of the writers. We can find only our own ideas about what those acts and that thinking must be. We are dependent on the Bible for the revelation.'[20] What we have in the Bible is the verbalization of the revelation in written form. In writing, ephemeral speech receives a permanent home. Indeed, the scriptures themselves, as W. J. Martin observes, recognize this function of writing (cf. e.g. Romans 4:3; 9:17; 10:11, etc.). In our law courts the validity of written words and documents is regarded as a substitute for the spoken word. In the case of the death of a testator the preference for a documentary will is a matter of plain common sense; one reason for this is that a written document excludes the necessity of an intermediary, whose *bona fides* in turn would have to be scrutinized. This is the important principle exemplified in the written scriptures.[21] As we examine the scriptures we are left in no doubt whatever that the vehicle of God's revelation to subsequent ages takes the form of the written word.

What God made known in past times he has not allowed to disappear into nothingness. If I have spoken, I cannot dissolve my speech. If what I say is faithfully recorded by someone, and I am subsequently confronted with it, I must acknowledge them as my words. In so far as the words spoken are the expression of my mind, the revelation of my thoughts, then in allowing that what is written is what I have said, I am declaring at the same time that what I *said* is what I *say*. In the scriptures, therefore, God's self-disclosure is recorded so that the record is one with the revelation. It is what God says. Such, rightly, was the way

Augustine regarded the Bible. As he affirms in his *Confessions*: '"What my scripture says," God declares, "I say."' So has the divine word been cast into permanent form in scripture which is itself the durable vehicle of God's self-disclosure providing for all time the conceptual framework in and through which man can meet and know God. 'The Bible is the witness to and the graphical residue of the divine act-word, the locus in which God's revealing activity now takes place.'[22]

The revelation of God in the old covenant was put into written form for the perpetual use of the people of God. But the provisions and promises of that Old Testament word reached their climax and fulfilment in the New.

> And if the redemptive purpose of God dictated that the revelation of the old covenant should be embodied in Scripture, can one doubt that the same divine purpose, as that came to far richer and glorious expression in the revelation of the new covenant, should contemplate that this revelation should likewise be incorporated in Scripture?[23]

There is indeed no doubt about the fact, since the New Testament is with us, everywhere bearing the marks of its inscripturation and so providing for the church the assured knowledge of the fulfilment of the divine purpose of redemption, and making it available for those who lay hold of it by faith. Although not ready, we think, to give the biblical record quite the same significance as is being argued for here, James Smart's statement is on the mark. The Bible, he declares,

> is indispensable if we are to know God and if we are to be in truth the body of the risen Lord because through it alone are we able to listen with Israel and with the apostolic church for the unique word out of the unseen which was for them, and can be for us, the power of God bringing our huma life to its fulfilment.[24]

Scripture and revelation

This identity of scripture with divine revelation is disliked by some modern theologians. It is repudiated, for example, by Brunner as a 'fatal equation' since it results in 'a theory of verbal inspiration as the basis of the divine authority of the Bible.'[25] But it is precisely on this coalescence of revelation with scripture that we are insisting. And if the concept of verbal inspiration follows, so be it, for, as we shall see, this is the sort of inspiration the Bible claims for itself. The cleavage between revelation and scripture for which Brunner and others contend has been illustrated by the use of the two Latin words, *revelatio* and *revelatum*. The first refers to the *act* of revealing itself; the second – *revelatum* – is the *result* of that revealing, the objective fact of the unveiling seen or heard. In the thought of these writers, *revelatio* is conceived as an immediate act of God in the present having the nature of a divine inbreaking. In this case all that a man can know are 'moments-of-God's revealing'. There is here no consequent *revelatum* – no deposit to which we can point and say, 'that is revelation.' And certainly in this view there is no inscripturated written record to which we can look for God's self-disclosure.

But this refusal to identify revelation with scripture is out of harmony with what the church throughout the ages believed about the biblical record. In its historical understanding the Bible is regarded as embodying the objective aspect of the divine self-disclosure in the verbal expression of language. In other words, God's *revelatio* in history has left behind its *revelatum* in scripture. We must, therefore, reject the notion that in the actual history God was at work revealing, but in the record or commentary it was man who did the construing, and that in the transfer to writing much of the reality has vanished or been obscured. We must repudiate the proposition of C. H. Dodd that the Bible contains the mere opinions of experts in the knowledge of God, masters in the art of living, the notions of religious geniuses.[26] This is far from the truth. It is the living God himself who speaks in the scriptures, speaks 'in, with, and under' the biblical word. 'For the Word that God speaks is alive and active; it cuts more keenly than any two-edged sword' (Hebrews 4:12, Phillips). And when it comes down to it, even those who have been most careful to refuse an identity between revelation and scripture find themselves unable to maintain the separation. Thus Brunner, whom we noted considered the equation 'fatal', forgets himself, and just over a dozen pages on affirms, 'Holy Scripture therefore does not only speak of the revelation; it is itself the revelation.'[27]

It is the whole scripture as the record of God's revealed acts and the God-given interpretation which together constitute the Bible the revelation of God. Both the events themselves and their record unite to make scripture the *revelatum*. Not that those who regard the Bible in this high manner imprison God in a book. Nor are they guilty of Bible-worship ('bibliolaters'), as the charge goes. God is no more imprisoned in a book than he was confined within any one past medium of his revealing. The book presents God to us; and by its means we both see and hear God – the living God. We do not regard the telescope put to the eye of the astronomer as a means of obstruction. It is rather the means of observation. By it is learned what, without it, could never be discovered. So is it with the written scriptures when focused by faith. By such means God's redemptive self-disclosure throughout history is brought to us and God himself in his saving activity is encountered.

3
THE WORD OF GOD

'Sir,' remarked Dr Johnson in the presence of the ever-faithful Boswell, 'ours is a book religion.' In spite of Hans Küng's blank denial, that 'Christianity is not a book religion. The Scriptures are not themselves divine revelation',[1] Johnson's assertion is in a certain and profound sense quite true. Christians have a book which records God's self-disclosure, which 'record is as a whole the revelation – God's complete word – for us.'[2] Throughout the ages the church has affirmed the divinity of its scriptures. The emphatic declaration has been consistent that the Bible is the word of God. And the *is* here has the absolute sense of identity: the Bible *is*, as an objective, written scripture, the word of God. Moses kept, in obedience to the divine command, the book of the law beside the ark. This juxtaposition of the book and the ark suggests that between the word of God and the church of God there is a perennial tie. They belong together. As stated in a pamphlet produced by the Committee of the Lambeth Conference in 1958, 'The Church must live by the Bible. More than that, it must know itself as the Church of the Bible, the people of God.'[3] The Bible is, then, the Book of the church; the document of the Christian faith. Ours is, indeed, a book religion.

To the Fathers of the post-apostolic church the divinity of the holy scriptures was axiomatic. But we need not produce here a long catena of such declarations; each would, in his own words, state the conviction of Augustine of Hippo, 'What is the Bible else but a letter of God Almighty addressed to his creatures, in which letter we hear the voice of God, and behold the heart of our Heavenly Father?' 'For Augustine and his hearers,' as Peter

Brown says, 'the Bible was literally the "word" of God. It was regarded as a single communication, a single message in an intricate code, and not as a heterogeneous collection of separate books.'[4]

The Reformation brought to a focus once again this valuation of the Bible as the word of God. For Calvin there is no equivocation: he directs man to the scriptures as the only source of true knowledge of God. Without the Bible man is left to mere glimmers and guesses: 'we must go, I say, to the word, where the character of God, drawn from his works, is declared accurately and to the life.'[5] For Luther no less than for Calvin the scriptures were the word of God. Although Heindrich Bornkamm notes that Luther 'was fond of calling Christ the Word of God because there is no more exact agency for self-communication than words,'[6] this did not prevent the great reformer (nor has it some of his followers) from giving the Bible the same designation. And this Luther does precisely, too, because 'there is no more exact agency for self-communication than words.' For Luther the identity of holy scripture with the word of God was generally assumed, and sometimes stated explicitly.[7] In fact the opening words of his *Table Talks* run thus: 'that the Bible is God's word and book I prove thus ...' For 'where do we find God's word except in the Scriptures?', he asks rhetorically elsewhere – asks so as to suggest the reply, 'Nowhere.'[8] And in his Schmalkaldic Articles he declares: 'The Word of God and nothing else shall establish an article of faith.'[9]

'God's word written'

The churches which grew out of the Reformation have stated a like conviction in their various confessions. Number twenty of the Thirty-nine Articles devised by the Church of England in 1562 states that the Bible is 'God's word written'. While the Westminster Confession of eighty-five years later affirms that since God, who is truth, is the author of scripture 'it ought to be received because it is the Word of God.' The Longer Catechism asks the question, 'What is the Word of God?' The answer given is, 'The Holy Scriptures of the Old and New Testaments are the Word of God, the only rule of faith and obedience.' For the Puritans, and their Evangelical successors, the same sure faith in the scriptures was constant.

Thomas Watson in *The Body of Divinity* regards the Bible as 'the sacred Book of God'. He then sets himself 'to prove this great truth, that the Scriptures are the very word of God'. To this end he marshals seven arguments in the manner of Calvin. There are the antiquity and marvellous preservation of the books. There is the matter they contain, the high truths regarding God and life too abstruse for man or angel to have hit upon. Watson points to the amazing impartiality of the several writers; and more specifically to the way some of them refused to cover up their own dark failings. 'What man who writes a history would black his own face, by recording those things of himself which might stain his reputation?' he asks. The power and efficacy of the word to transform human life is another strong argument for the Bible's divinity. And, of course, there are also the evidence of prophecy and the instances of specific miracles by which God sets his seal of approval upon scripture as his own.[10] To Charles Simeon, the Bible was an inspired volume 'with nothing superfluous, nothing defective,' and thus to 'be *wholly* and *exclusively* called "the Word of God".'[11]

For John Wesley, God's special revelation is equated with the Bible as the oracles of God.[12] 'I really believe the Bible to be the Word of God', he says with evident emphasis. Wesley was sure that he possessed a divine book, and he adduces four arguments designed to prove it the word of God.[13]

But does the scripture give warrant for this high valuation of itself as 'the word of God?' The phrase certainly does occur numerous times in the Old Testament, and throughout the record the declarations of the 'Law', the 'Prophets' and the 'Psalms' are referred directly to God. The meaning of the term 'word' (Hebrew *dabar*) is set for us at the beginning. In Genesis, God's word is his active forthcoming. 'God said,' 'And it was so,' (Genesis 1:24). Such is God's word – a word of power, of faithfulness, of fulfilment. God's word expresses his character. God is what he says. Thus is his word creating (Psalm 33:6), healing

(Psalm 107:20), quickening (Psalm 119:25), and strengthening (Psalm 119:28).

> Because it is God's word [says Kittel] it is an active and energizing word; it is not only an indication (*Hinweis*) of grace, salvation, life, but it works salvation and life, because it is grace, salvation, and life – James 1:21 – the word ... which is able to save your souls.[14]

The phrase the 'word of God' may be taken, therefore, to underlie a conviction. Lawgiver, prophet, and psalmist of the Old Testament believed themselves to have received their communication from God. And in the records, which in many cases they were commanded by God to write, the word of God was preserved (cf. e.g. Exodus 17:14; 24:4; Joshua 1:8; 1 Kings 2:3; 2 Chronicles 35:12; Jeremiah 30:3; 45:1; Habakkuk 2:2, etc.). From Genesis to Malachi, one after another asserts his conviction that he declares the word of God. So constant throughout the Old Testament are such phrases as 'the word of God' or, 'of the Lord', or that 'God spake', or 'God said', that it can confidently be asserted that the whole is dominated by the claim. In fact the phrase 'Thus says the Lord' or its equivalent occurs nearly 4,000 times in the Old Testament. Both in their origin and in their preservation are the words of the Law and the Prophets attributed to God. The biblical conception of the Old Testament is, therefore, that of a divinely communicated word.

After this fashion the writers of the New Testament regarded the Old. To quote it was to affirm the utterance of God. It was, indeed, indifferent whether the quotation was prefaced, 'God spake', or 'the scripture says'. Warfield draws attention to the habit of the New Testament writers of equating God and scripture. They sometimes appeal to the scripture as if it were God giving the verdict directly (cf. Galatians 3:8 (cf. Genesis 12:13); Romans 9:17 (cf. Exodus 9:16)); on other occasions they appeal to God as if he were scripture personified (cf. Matthew 19:4, 5 (cf. Genesis 2:24); Hebrews 3:7 (cf. Psalm 95:7); Acts 4:24, 25 (cf. Psalm 2:1); Acts 13:34, 35 (cf. Isaiah 55:3)). The Epistle to the Hebrews is especially instructive and illuminating in this connection. Concerning the Mosaic rites it is affirmed that 'this the Holy Spirit indicates' (9:8). The prophecy of Jeremiah is quoted, and enforced with the declaration, 'the Holy Spirit also bears witness.' In the third chapter the writer uses as a clinching argument a passage from Psalm 92, but the words are attributed to the Holy Spirit – 'Therefore, as the Holy Spirit says, "Today, if you shall hear his word, . . ." ' (verse 7). For the New Testament authors, the Old Testament embodied the word of God, while the whole canon of Old Testament scripture was regarded as the word of God written.

But not only does the phrase *the word of God* underline a conviction, it also introduces a contrast. Throughout the Old Testament the designation 'the word of God' stands over against all that is earthly and human. In contrast with flower and flesh which fade and fail is the word of God which abides for ever (Isaiah 40:6–8; cf. 1 Peter 1:24, 25). Therefore is God's word firmly fixed in the heavens (cf. Psalm 119:89), as 'right' (Psalm 33:4), 'true' (Psalm 119:160), and 'good' (Isaiah 39:8). It is in the 'word' (*imrah*) that man is upheld (Psalm 119:116), and by which are his ways ordered (Psalm 119:133). For it is through the word that God comes to man as personal; and in that act of God's free self-giving man finds his own genuine selfhood as created in the divine image. In the Old Testament, then, 'the word is the supreme means by which God the Creator makes both himself known and his will to his creatures.'[15] The word of God brought the world into being and created history. And the word of the Lord came as a sure word of prophecy, confronting the people of the time with both warning and command. To the Psalmist the word of the Lord is to be trusted (Psalm 119:42) as the giver of light (Psalm 119:105), life (Psalm 119:25), and understanding (Psalm 119:169). It is in this contrast with all that is passing, imperfect, and human that the word of the Lord is declared to be 'pure' (Psalm 12:6), and 'perfect' (Psalm 19:7).

But what of the New Testament? How are we to understand its connection with the word of God?

The New Testament

We may begin our answer to these questions by pointing out that the designation 'the word of God' occurs in three main contexts in the New Testament. There is, first, the term 'word' used in an absolute sense, as in John 1:1f. 'The Word became flesh.' In the person of Jesus Christ, John is affirming, God's mind with regard to man was made actual, comprehensive, and historical. As the Word – the Logos – Christ was among men as the incarnate speech of God; and as such he communicates to those who receive him, who believe in him, eternal life. John sees the existence of the Word carried beyond the limits of time; and he stresses both his separate personality – 'the Word was with God,' and his true deity, – 'the Word was God.' The Word did not become personal or divine either before the creation or in the incarnation. In coming to be what he was, he did not come to be what he was not. The absolute eternal relations of the persons of the Godhead furnish the basis for the revelation which is declared to be in the Word made flesh. Precisely because the Word was personally distinct from God, and yet essentially God, he could make God known. In speaking of Christ as the Word, John is making use of a term which expresses his absolute nature as God. In him, as the Word made flesh, the eternal self-revealing God became incarnate.

There are two other references to Christ as the Word in the Johannine literature. In 1 John 1:1 there is the equation of the incarnate one with 'the word of life'. As *the word of life* he was seen, heard and handled by his apostles; for such was the actuality of his presence in the world. In Christ, as the word of life, the very life of God was encountered. In Revelation 19:13 there is the specific designation 'the Word of God' in reference to the exalted Jesus. As the Word of God, he is the Lamb and the Lion; and King of kings, and Lord of lords. (Revelation 19:16.)

There is a second use of the phrase 'the word of God' in the New Testament. The preached message of the gospel is spoken of in such terms. There was a time when the New Testament as we have it today was not in existence. But 'the word of God' was there – the saving message of Christ. The early disciples spoke this 'word of God' with boldness (Acts 4:29), and thus did 'the word of God' increase (Acts 6:7). The Book of Acts is, in fact, strewn with references to the proclamation and progress of the apostolic preaching of 'the word of God'. And throughout Acts, as in Romans and 2 Peter, this word of apostolic preaching is identified with the essential 'word of God' of the Old Testament. The word of God proclaimed orally by its first witnesses is one and the same with the 'word' finally embodied in written form in the New Testament.

We are thus led on to the third use of the term to designate in principle the scriptures themselves. It is used in this fashion, for example, by our Lord in John 10:35. Scripture, as 'the word of God', he affirms, cannot be broken; it cannot be 'set aside' (NEB). Obviously the reference here cannot in the first instance be to the New Testament writings. But in specifying 'scripture', Jesus was indicating a certain type of literature, namely, that which is 'canonical', and as such normative for faith. Into this category the New Testament eventually came. The New Testament writers frequently use the phrase 'the word of God' for the divine revelation preserved in the Old Testament. They regarded the message of the gospel as being the true meaning of the former Testament. For Moses, and all the prophets, they had learned from their Lord, wrote of Christ (Luke 24:27); and those prophets, sometimes, according to 1 Peter 1:11, without full awareness of it, spoke of him under the direct influence of the Holy Spirit. Thus did the New Testament writers identify the word of God, which they equated with the Old Testament scriptures, with their own word, as being equally 'the word of God'. They never regarded themselves as merely offering spiritual advice or making useful suggestions, or stating good ideas. They believed themselves to be occupied with divine issues. So, for example, does Mark declare his interest in the gospel of Jesus Christ, the Son of God, and right away refer to what is written in the prophets (Mark 1:1, 2). And John asserts that the things he writes are to the end that we may believe that Jesus is the Christ, the Son of God, and that believing we may have life in his name (John 20:31). Paul, too, declares that what he writes is a command of the Lord (cf. 1 Corinthians 14:37); things, in fact, revealed by God's Spirit (cf. 1 Corinthians 2:10). As many therefore, as John Macleod says,

who are willing to sit at the feet of the Apostles, as they thus by their written word continue to bear witness and to teach, will treat the Old Testament Scriptures as it is plain the Lord and his Apostles did. They will accept both Testaments as the Word of God.'[15]

So is the word of God by the mouth of his prophets and apostles the word of God to *me*. For 'what makes the Bible pre-eminently the Word of God' is 'the direct application of the eternal Word to one's own soul.'[16]

When, therefore, as soon happened (cf. 2 Peter 3:16), the first Christian believers began to accept certain of their writings as Scripture, it was with the connotation, the *word of God*, which was for them an alternative designation for the Old Testament. Between the two Testaments there was no cleavage in this matter. When, for example, in New Testament days those of the first church referred to Christ as Lord (*kurios*) they did it with full understanding of its Old Testament application to God himself. And they did not hesitate to make the equation. So, too, is it with the term scripture. The Old Testament was accepted in the conviction that it was the word of God. Thus, when the title 'scripture' came to be applied to the writings which go to form our New Testament, it was with a significance not different from, but identical with, how the word was understood in relation to the Old. To the early believers what was scripture was the word of God. The writings were the 'oracles of God' (cf. Acts 7:38; Romans 3:2; Hebrews 5:12; 1 Peter 4:11). They were in a vital and valid sense the utterances of the Lord. By an inescapable logic the New Testament writings carry the designation the word of God. For what is scripture is the word of God; and the New Testament is scripture, so is it the word of God. And on this there was not, then, and should not be now, the least equivocation. For if 'the Word that is God's was to come to all men, then there had to be such a process in which preached and written words mediate belief in the risen Lord.'[17]

Thus the designation 'the Word of God', or 'the word of God', refers in particular to Jesus Christ; in general to the gospel message; and, in principle, to the New Testament writings themselves. It has these three distinct meanings. Yet these three are not unrelated. They do in fact actually lie one within the other as concentric circles. Christ himself is the ultimate, the total Word. He is, therefore, for us men and our salvation the normative expression of God, and is consequently the Word in an absolute sense. But this Word is expounded and given completed interpretation in the New Testament scriptures, which fact thus makes it total and final as the word of God. For the early church the Old Testament, read from the standpoint of the Word made flesh, was the word of God. This was the message proclaimed – the word of God's salvation in Christ – by the apostolic preachers; and as such it was unequivocally, for these chosen witnesses, God's word. In summary, then, we can say that the phrase 'the word of God' refers to God's own revelation of himself made known personally in Christ, preached by the apostolic witnesses, and embodied in written form in the New Testament scriptures. For the apostles did not claim themselves to be wise men discoursing on God. Rather, as Gabriel Morgan declares, was their claim much simpler and more startling.

> They claimed to speak *in* Christ, to have been given the Spirit which enabled them to speak from within the mystery of God. Their words were put forth not as human words on a divine truth, but as words which would bring the believer face to face with Christ (Galatians 3:1) and convey to the believer a share in the wisdom proper to the Son (Philippians 2:5). The word that issued from this life in Christ and the word that mediated this knowledge was thus spoken of as the 'word of God'.[18]

It is therefore vital to note the overlapping of these three connotations of the term in the New Testament itself. There are numerous passages where *the word of God* can be referred with equal right to the spoken or the written word (cf. Matthew 7:13; Luke 8:21; Acts 4:31; 6:7; 12:24; 13:5, 7, 44; 18:11; 19:20; Romans 9:6; 2 Corinthians 4:2; 1 Thessalonians 2:13; 1 Timothy 4:5; 2 Timothy 2:9; Titus 2:5; Hebrews 13:7; 1 John 2:14, etc.). On the other hand, there are some passages in the New Testament where a specific life-giving quality is attributed to the 'word', but it is not altogether clear whether the reference is to the incarnate or written word.

In Philippians 2:16, for example, there is the expression 'the word of life' (*logos zoen*); the title seems here to be applied to the written word. But the same expression is given in John 1 to Christ himself (*ho logos . . . en auto zoe ēn*). Thus are the written word and the Word incarnate so identified that we are not always sure to which reference is made. The fundamental resemblance lies in that both are a tangible expression of the invisible God. As the written or spoken word expresses, for the purposes of communicating to another, the invisible and inaccessible thought, so Jesus Christ, as the incarnate Word and the scriptures as the written word, express and communicate knowledge of the invisible and inaccessible God.

In Hebrews 4:12 there is the statement, 'For the word of God is alive and active. It cuts more keenly than any two-edged sword' (NEB). Commentators disagree as to whether this refers to the incarnate or written word. On the whole it seems to suit the writer's thought better to take it to mean the word as written. Yet the very next verse unites the incarnate Word, who searches human hearts, with the action of the written word. In 1 Peter 1:23 it is difficult again to decide whether the incarnate or written word is in view. Peter speaks of 'the permanent word of the living God' (Phillips). More probably the reference is to the written word in view of the following quotation from Isaiah 40:6–8. But nonetheless an action is attributed to it which is elsewhere referred to the incarnate Word. We may then conclude with J. K. Mozley that 'in the Christian view of the Bible, it is finally true that it is the Word of God, just as it is finally true about Christ that He is the Word of God.'[19]

The Bible is the word of God: such is the verdict to which our considerations have led us. And this verdict has the certain witness and warrant of the Bible itself.

Other views

In recent times a number of views have been put forth, each with its own key-word, but agreeing in initiating a divorce, or at most a nebulous connection, between the Bible and the word of God. Some consider that the Bible only 'contains' the word of God: others that it actually 'becomes' the word of God when God chooses so to use it; and some others that it merely 'points' to the word of God, which is other than, and beyond, itself. All these ideas had their origin in the immediate post-Darwinian period when the Bible was thought of by many simply as giving a highly interesting account of man's progressive discovery of God. In the context of what came to be known as the Higher Criticism which followed directly from the Darwinian evolutionism they came to full bloom.

F. W. Farrar appears to have been among the first to popularize the view in this country that 'Scripture *contains* the Word of God.'[20] Dean Farrar goes so far as to contend that the declaration of the Church of England that the Bible 'is' the word of God is 'an accident'. If we will, we may speak of the Bible as a whole as the word of God; but only 'because it contains words and passages of God to the human soul; but it is not in its whole extent, and throughout, identical with the Word of God.'[21] Quite a host of writers lined up behind Farrar; and one after another censured those who dared to proclaim the historic faith that the Bible *is* the word of God. A. S. Peake played the same tune as the Dean of Canterbury. To hold that the Bible is the word of God, Peake trumpeted, is to be committed to 'the high-sounding' but 'impossible' theory, that 'from the beginning to the end the Bible was dictated by the Holy Spirit himself to selected men each of whom acted as His amanuensis. Nothing in it has a human origin, the book was wholly divine in all its parts.'[22] At a later date A. G. Hebert in *Fundamentalism and the Church of God* (1957) took up the same position, going so far as to condemn the declaration that the Bible is the word of God as a grave menace to the church of God.

Dr James Packer has, however, shown how unreasonable, unhistorical and unscriptural is this divorce between the Bible and the word of God. He declares rightly, 'When we call the Bible the Word of God, we mean, or should mean, that its message constitutes a single utterance of which God is the author.'[23] The trouble with the view that the Bible 'contains' the word of God only is the difficulty of deciding which passage speaks of God. It is, in fact, impossible to distinguish in any given passage some short sentence out of the whole as having a divine character above the rest. It is because the Bible, despite its great variety, is an organic unity that we must accept it as a whole. Throughout it there is to be heard the notes of one divine music. This means, as L. S. Thornton says, that 'It is not enough to say that the Word of God is contained *in* the Scriptures. We must insist once more that the Scripture *is* the Word of God.'[24]

Insistence upon scripture as in itself and objectively the word of God does not mean that the formula, the Bible contains the word of God, is to be discarded as absolutely false. When used in its proper context, and with right understanding, the statement may stand. It is to be rejected if it is understood as insinuating that part of what the Bible contains is no part of the word of God. But if the two formulae are taken together as complementary they are acceptable. To say that the Bible 'is' the word of God without qualification is to lose sight of the fact that it contains the words of men, and even of devils, which are not true in themselves. On the other hand, to limit belief to the phrase that the Bible 'contains' the word of God only, calls for an impossible attempt to discriminate between what is God's word and what is not. We may then conclude with James Denney that

> the Bible *is* the word of God in the sense that it conveys to us an accurate record of everything God intended man to know in connection with his will. The Bible *contains* the word of God in the sense that in it is enshrined the word of God which is revealed to us for our redemption.'[25]

Among those championing the idea that the Bible 'becomes' the word of God in experience are Barth and Brunner, and quite recently Hans Küng.[26] We have alluded earlier to Barth's insistence on a divorce between revelation and the biblical record. This separation he carries through consistently to conclude that between the scripture and the word of God there is no absolute connection. It is at most a 'witness' to God's revelation in Christ, the Word disclosed in the moment of encounter. The same general position is maintained by Emil Brunner. He, too, separates Christ as the Word from the Bible as human testimony to God's revelation. He regards the scriptures as the 'bearer' of God's word. Yet not every part is so in the same way, or to the same extent.[27] Some passages, indeed, but 'stammer' out his name.[28] That which is on the 'rim' of the New Testament has little possibility of becoming the word of God to us; while other passages, such as 2 Peter 2:4, are quite outside the 'rim'. It is, in the famous words of S. T. Coleridge, when a passage 'finds me' that it becomes the word of God to me. Brunner likens the Voice of God in the Bible to 'His Master's Voice', or to a voice heard on a gramophone record. It is the real voice of the singer which is heard, but there are noises and scratchings besides, which are no part of the master's voice.[29]

This analogy proffered by Brunner is all right as far as it goes, but it does not well suit Brunner's own view. For how can we really be sure that the voice we hear is indeed the master's voice? Just when it 'finds' us, we are assured. But is there truly any assurance in that? And, after all, according to both Barth and Brunner, there are parts of the record which are not tuned to the master's voice and can never *bear* his message. By what criterion, then, do we separate the other voices on the record from the master's voice? It is all too difficult; indeed, impossible.

C. H. Dodd insists that in the expression 'the Word of God' there 'lurks an equivocation.'[30] The Bible is that which *points to* God's revelation. And we can only know that the word of God has come to us in experience. For 'the criterion lies within ourselves.'[31] Nowhere, he declares, is the truth given in such purely 'objective' form that we can find a self-subsistent external authority.[32] Although wishing to give the Bible some sort of status by hedging it about with such statements as its being the Document of the Covenant, Dodd's ultimate view of the Bible is that of a human book.

If, however, Dodd hesitates to say explicitly what is the logic of his own assessment of the Bible, James Barr has no such inhibition. He complains that the traditional habit of referring the Bible directly to God obscures the fact that it is essentially 'a human work'. It is a record of man's beliefs, experiences, and stories of religion. Concepts like the word of God he thinks inappropriate. And so he asserts: 'If one wants to use the Word-of-God type of language, the proper term for the Bible would be Word of Israel, Word of some leading early Christians.'[33] But does Barr know better than the biblical writers themselves the

source of their own communications? The prophets of the Old
Testament were sure they were recording *God's* word for Israel;
and leading New Testament Christians like Paul believed
themselves to be stating *God's* word for the churches.

Perhaps we have been too punctilious in distinguishing
between the views that the Bible *contains,* or *becomes,* or *points to*
the word of God. All of them want very much to say the same
thing, and make the same distinction by denying to the Bible as
such the designation *the word of God.* But each formula taken on
its own is equally false. It would be queer to assert that water
contains H_2O, and queerer still to insist that it becomes H_2O as it
is drunk; and queerest of all to say that it points to H_2O. Each of
these contentions would have only a semblance of sense if it is
understood that water itself *is* a combination of hydrogen and
oxygen in their proper proportions. So is it with the Bible. The
prior and necessary declaration is that *the Bible is the word of God.*

The Old Testament is a God-given book indeed: and, of
course, the New Testament no less. For all men this Bible of
both Testaments is objectively the word of God whether they
are awakened to it or not, found by it or not. But to the faith-
awakened it contains the word, and becomes the word in living
experience, and, as the written word, points to him who is the
Word of God incarnate. When, then, as F. F. Bruce says, 'we
speak of the *Scriptures* we use a word which etymologically
denotes the writing and not the material.' Without writing, he
adds, there would be no Bible at all, 'for the Bible is God's Word
written.'[34]

Put then in a lapidary statement, the position is this: if we have
no sure word of God we have no 'saving knowledge'. Nor would
there be any spiritual interest or benefit, therefore, in seeking out
what the Bible teaches. There would be no living and eternal
concern in reflecting on the self-disclosure of God which the
scriptures claim to be present; there would, that is to say, be no
theology of the word. For, as Moltmann has said,

> Theology as *speaking about God* is possible only on the basis of *what
> God himself says.* Theology as the reflection of faith upon the word
> received assumes the event of the word spoken by God himself.
> Faith can claim to be in accord with rational understanding only in

so far as it understands what God says. And this understanding consists of considering the word of God in constant awareness that God is the subject of everything which theology considers, and in attentiveness to the word of God as it is uttered. The *theology of faith* presupposes the *theology of God*, which is found in the word of God which has been and which is uttered.'[35]

4

THE INSPIRED BOOK

We have seen in a previous chapter that, while a distinction may be made between God's revelatory self-disclosure and its consequent record, the two – revelation and record – are nevertheless so dovetailed that we are compelled to say with James Orr that '*the record*, in the fullness of its contents, *is itself for us the revelation.*'[1] In fact, some elements of God's revelation, such as sections of the Old Testament message and the New Testament epistles, were given in written form from the first. And these, together with other features of God's unveiling which were later put in written form, constitute God's complete and completed revelation. And the sufficiency of this revelation is shown by the fact the we do not have to travel beyond the biblical record to find God's whole will for man.

In the record, then, God's revelation is permanently secured. But if God has seen fit to secure his revelation in record, then we cannot but believe that he would have regard to the *way* it should be done. It would be monstrous to suppose that God should give a revelation of himself and leave it to man to record it *ad lib.* It is hardly credible to conceive that God, who in grace made known to man the sum of saving knowledge, was then unable or unwilling to preserve the recorders thereof, in a manner worthy of himself, so as to make their record a trustworthy bearer of his self-disclosure. We cannot believe that God, having performed his miraculous revelatory acts, and having illuminated the minds of prophets and apostles to understand their saving import, left the prophetic and apostolic testimony to take care of itself. This would indeed be a strange view of divine providence; a view inconsistent with the God revealed, which would deny to the biblical writers that necessary divine aid in their endeavours to preserve for the world that revelation which, for the world's sake, had been communicated to them.

The truth is, however, that God *has* acted, not only in revelation, but also in a way fitting for the perpetuation of that revelation. This manner of his acting is what is understood as divine inspiration. In revelation we have God's way of self-disclosure, his supernatural interposition into the human situation for man's redemption; in inspiration we have God's supernatural moving of chosen men to secure, in permanent form, what he has said and done that men may be redeemed.

But revelation and inspiration do not in every instance coalesce. For there can be revelation without inspiration, and inspiration without revelation. Revelation has to do with the disclosure of divine truth; inspiration with its communication. So God may give a revelation to one and move another to record it. Thus, for example, the Josephs of both Testaments received a divine disclosure in the form of dreams, but neither was commissioned to record it. On the other hand, there can be inspiration without revelation. The letters of heathen kings are in themselves no divine disclosure; nor, for example in the New Testament, is the oration of the town clerk of Ephesus (Acts 19:35f.). But the biblical writers were inspired of God to use their material. In the case of a writer such as Luke there is no evidence of an individual divine communication made to him. The beloved doctor himself marshalled the facts; but he was most certainly moved, guarded, and guided by the Spirit of God in the assessing and recording of these facts for the continued blessing and benefit of the church of God in all subsequent ages. The inspired recorders of God's revelation presented facts with that reality of accuracy which only divine inspiration could secure; but not always did they themselves receive their facts by a direct revelation. Yet most certainly did they record them under the direct action of God's Spirit.

God's special revelation, then, finds its perpetuation in the scriptural record, while the record itself shows evidence of God's inspiration. This means that 'the validity and nature of biblical inspiration rest on the credentials and shape of revelation'.[2] And God's revelation we have in scripture; which scripture every·

where declares itself as God's word. Constant in the biblical record are such declarations as 'God spake', or 'God has spoken', by the word of a prophet or a psalmist. Thus God says to Jeremiah, 'Behold, I have put my words in your mouth' (Jeremiah 1:9), and to Ezekiel, 'And you shall speak my words to them' (Ezekiel 2:7). And David also says, 'The Spirit of the Lord spake by me, his word was upon my tongue' (2 Samuel 23:2). Such assertions could be multiplied to show it to be the unmistakable testimony of scripture that the utterances of its several spokesmen function as the mouthpiece of the Holy Spirit. Indeed, in its biblical conception and connotation, the prophet is essentially the man whose mouth utters the words of God. For the Old Testament prophets were, as Clement of Alexandria insists, 'organs of the divine voice.'[3] No less were the New Testament apostles so to whom Jesus declared the words of the Father. And the biblical word revealed is the same word as recorded. For this reason can Paul personify scripture as God speaking (cf. Romans 9:17; Galatians 3:8). This personification of scripture can only be explained because the apostle identifies scripture and the word of God.[4]

In a true sense it can then be said that God is the author of the biblical word (cf. Acts 13:32–35). All this means that scripture is persuasive throughout with the reality of a supernatural inspiration. And the proof of this reality of supernatural inspiration is not based upon a few texts of the Bible itself, although there are a couple of passages, as we shall see, in which the fact is specifically declared. The truth is rather that the scripture carries everywhere the stamp of the divine impulse. So omnipresent, indeed, is the evidence of the Spirit's relation to the written word that the only reason for the failure to apprehend it would seem to be disbelief in the scripture's own claim to be the word of God. 'It may surprise those who have not looked into the subject with care', says James Orr, 'to discover how strong, full, and persuasive, the testimony of Scripture to its own inspiration is.'[5] But the scriptures can only be looked into 'with care', if there is genuine care for the subject. It is only the Spirit resident in the heart which can testify to the Spirit's relation to the word. As Gabriel Morgan says, 'Only to the mind living in the conditions of the covenant does Scripture surrender its meaning.'[6]

The ultimate ground, however, for accepting scripture as divinely inspired is the authority of Christ our Lord. For as J. W. Wenham declares, 'Belief in Christ as the supreme revelation of God leads to belief in scriptural revelation – of the Old Testament by the direct testimony of Jesus and of the New Testament by inference from his testimony.'[7] All scripture, Christ asserts, spoke of him; he is both its true context and its full content.

> There can be no doubt that for Jesus the Old Testament was authoritative, that he himself heard in it the very word of God himself and that he regarded its authors as speaking through the inspiration of the Holy Spirit.[8]

He who declared that 'My teaching is not mine but his who sent me' (John 7:16; cf. 12:48–50) made the same claim for scripture as he made for his own word, that it 'shall not pass away' (cf. Matthew 24:35; John 10:35). 'The significance of this fact is great,' comments Clark Pinnock. 'He on whom the salvation of men depends taught with the greatest of force the full inspiration of extant Scripture. He regarded God as its true Author, and bowed to its divine authority.'[9] Peter quotes the psalmist's affirmation that 'the word of the Lord abides forever', and immediately identifies that word of the Lord with the 'good news which was preached' by the apostolic messengers (1 Peter 1:25, 26).

The process of inspiration

Coming to treat more specifically with what is to be understood by divine inspiration, we will contend that in any true account of it, both the action of God upon the writers, and the result of that action in the scriptural record, must receive effective statement.

We shall begin, then, by defining inspiration as that direct influence of God upon the writers of the Bible in such a manner that, while they did not cease to be themselves, they were so moved, guarded, and guided by the Holy Spirit that their resulting productions constitute the one all-sufficient word of God for men.

That this is no new doctrine and strange could be easily demonstrated. It is the true and historic faith. It is not the property of a few ultra-orthodox individuals, but rather the settled conviction of the universal Church of Christ from its first planting. Whatever the divine scripture says, declares Gregory of Nyssa in the fourth century, 'is the voice of the Holy Spirit'. The language of the Bible, observes Justin Martyr at an earlier date, is 'the very language of God'. In these two statements we have in sum what the scripture has to say about its own inspiration – it is 'of the Holy Spirit' and is in 'language' which is of God.

The first fact that confronts us when we consider the subject of inspiration is that the scriptures show themselves to be at the same time obviously a human and evidently a divine product. The command given to Baruch may be said to cover its several writings. Baruch wrote from the mouth of Jeremiah all the words of the Lord, which had been spoken unto him, upon the roll of a book (cf. Jeremiah 36; 45:1, 2). The mouth was Jeremiah's; the writing was Baruch's; the words upon the scroll were the words of the Lord.

There is no need to adduce proof of the Bible's human authorship. Each writer has his own style and reveals his own idiosyncrasies. But no less sure are the indications of God as the *auctor primarius* of scripture, or, perhaps, we should say that God by the process of inspiration is the direct author of scripture. It is, therefore, indifferent whether, for example, we affirm, 'David spake', or 'the Holy Spirit spake', or whether it is declared that 'God says' or 'the scripture says'. 'No one but God,' observes Karl Rahner, 'can become an author by making someone else an author. For no one but God can arouse and direct man's free activity in such wise that his freedom is not thereby diminished, but actively constituted and made most itself.'[10] Throughout the Bible there is clearly this 'duality' of authorship: not the human to the exclusion of the divine; and not the divine to the exclusion of the human. Nor yet the one successive of the other. From first to last, what we have in the

Bible is God at work through man, and man at work for God, in such a way that both are wholly present in every word of scripture.

There can be no acceptable and sufficient account of inspiration which does not give adequate admission to this double aspect – to the divine and the human, to the Spirit and the letter. In the combination of these the very essence of the process of inspiration consists. The relation between the divine and the human is certainly not easy to understand, but to it all genuine Christian experience bears abundant witness. Of the possibility, indeed of the actuality, of such a combination the believing man has his own awareness. And the combination of divine and human in inspiration is but a special instance of this interplay for a particular purpose.

What we can understand by this inspiration of the Bible may become clearer if the issues involved are considered positively and negatively. The positive aspects are brought out in the emphasis in our definition upon inspiration as a process and a product. The *process* is the action of the Spirit of God whereby the biblical writers were 'moved, guarded, and guided.' The *product* is the scripture, as God's word written. And these two aspects are given special statement in the Bible itself.

As regards the first aspect of inspiration, the statement is made in 2 Peter 1:21 that it was 'not through any human whim that men prophesied of old; men they were, but, impelled by the Holy Spirit, they spoke the words of God' (NEB). The Greek word translated 'impelled' (AV, RSV 'moved') is *phero* which means literally 'borne along'. The word holds within it the idea of a secret and special influence of the Holy Spirit on these chosen men which resulted in their production of inspired scriptures. The thought is that the Spirit of God bore these men along as the wind catches the sails of a boat and carries it on before it. There are, then, as Warfield has shown, strong overtones in the term used by Peter. That which is 'borne' is taken up by the 'bearer' and conveyed by the 'bearer's' own power to the 'bearer's' designed goal. In this case the power to carry and the goal attained are of the Holy Spirit. 'True, this passage,' as Berkouwer observes, 'deals with prophecy, with the speaking of prophets (*alalesan*). Yet, this statement has always been related to the God-breathed character of Scripture.'[11] Peter is specifically emphasizing the divine origin of scripture (cf. 1 Peter 1:23–25). The Spirit of God spoke through the prophets (1 Peter 1:11) as he did also through Paul the apostle (cf. 2 Peter 3:16). The idea of men being energized by the Spirit of God runs through the Old Testament (cf. Micah 3:8; Zechariah 7:12). Amos speaks for them all when he declares, 'The Lord God has spoken, who can but prophesy?' (3:8; cf. Numbers 11:25; 1 Samuel 10:6–10; 2 Samuel 23:2; Nehemiah 9:30, etc.). It was indeed the very Spirit of Christ which brought the divine word to the prophets in ancient times. What men of God spoke in other days is what is for us divine scripture. While stating that it was the prophets who uttered the word, Peter is stressing that the word was initiated by the Spirit of God. Thus did their work have 'a divine stamp upon it. For they were moved by the Spirit, and their word was endowed with singular power and truthfulness.'[12]

The product of inspiration

So much for the process of the divine revelation; now something about the *product* of this action of the Holy Spirit. The product is the scripture as written; the revelation as recorded. Inspiration is not primarily something done *on* man, nor yet is it merely done *in* man. In our definition we have sought to focus attention on the writings themselves as something done *by* man, and at the same time something done so decisively by God that the result of the work done is rightly to be designated God's word written.

This is the point made conclusively in 2 Timothy 3:15–17. The first thing to note is the confession made here. Paul declares that it is the 'holy scriptures' which are able to make wise unto salvation through faith in Christ Jesus. The phrase *hiera grammata* is peculiar as a designation for the divine word. But there can be no doubt about the sense, as we know from Josephus and Philo that the term refers to the collection of sacred writings. The phrase itself emphasizes two facts. The first specifies the location of this saving. It is *grammata*; that is to say, the word that makes wise unto salvation is written. The other term indicates its nature. It is described as 'sacred' or 'holy'. The word 'holy' originally meant 'set apart'; it then took on an ethical connotation. Thus 'holy' came to refer to a specific relationship with God. The written word is, then, 'holy' because set apart and separated from other writings as having to do with God. It is consequently 'God's book' – the word of God written.

The second fact made clear in this passage is the conception that is here given to the recorded revelation. Paul has spoken collectively of the *hiera grammata* – the holy scriptures. He now speaks individually of the component parts, and declares that 'all scripture is inspired of God', or, as some versions have it, 'every scripture inspired of God'. It matters not, however, which translation is preferred. For there can be no scripture which is not inspired of God. It is inspiration which gives it inscripturation. In the passage the apostle now uses the term *graphe*: and in every place where this word occurs, whether singular or plural, with or without the article, it always denotes the sacred writings.

What then is being declared is that every piece of writing which makes up the sacred volume is inspired by God. The actual word for this inspiration used by the apostle is *theopneustos*, which means literally 'God-breathed'. By using such a term Paul is telling us that the sacred scriptures are not just inspiring. Other books may be that. And he is not even talking of their *in*spiration. We could say that other writings were the product of a flash of inspiration, like, for example, the poems of Wordsworth. If we characterize other literature as inspired the term is used in a secondary sense.

> It is journalistic and not a scientific use of the term. Even such a mode of speech lends a certain distinction to the Bible because it suggests an implicit comparison with sacred scripture. It refers all other books to the Bible as the standard.[13]

Nonetheless the scriptures are not just a type of ordinary writings 'breathed into by God'; nor are they the mere outcome of the divine 'inbreathing'. Rather are they the produce of God's own creative breath; and thus are they a divine product. Just as it is declared that 'by the word of God were the heavens made and the host of them by the breath of his mouth' (Psalm 33:6), so by God's 'out-breathing' were the scriptures produced. God's breath is the irresistible outflow of his power; and the scriptures are, therefore, the result of his life-giving action. As God breathed out life into man, and man became a living soul bearing his image, so God breathed out through man the words which alone are able to make wise unto salvation and instruct in the ways of righteousness. The book consequently carries God's image and superscription.

Bringing, then, these two passages together – 2 Peter 1:21, with its 'borne along', and 2 Timothy 3:16, with the phrase 'God-breathed' – we have this conclusion concerning the process and the product of inspiration. The men who were chosen to record God's revelation were carried along by the Holy Spirit so that there is secured through them a divinely communicated statement of the divine mind and will made known in his self-disclosure.

From first to last, both in the process and the product, God was with these chosen men, so that both in their receiving the word from him and their consequent declaring of it to others by speaking or writing, they accomplished their end in a way unattainable by their own insight, experience, or knowledge, but only as a result of the Holy Spirit's action in and through them.

The context of these declarations of the New Testament is the scriptures of the Old Testament. But it could be demonstrated that the New Testament claims an equal inspiration for itself. Christ promised his apostles the Holy Spirit to bring his word to their remembrance. The Thessalonians heard and received the apostolic word, not as the word of men, but, as it is in truth, the word of God (1 Thessalonians 1:13). Paul gives the Corinthians the commandments of the Lord. When, as in 2 Peter, that apostle puts the epistles of Paul on a level with 'the other scriptures', the connotation of the word was understood; scripture was 'from God' and was held to be a product of a special action of the divine Spirit.

Two important facts emerge from these considerations. First, the inspiration of the scriptures is truly *plenary*: it is full, entire, complete, such that all scripture, and scripture in all its parts, is

God-breathed. God was concerned that his revelation be preserved entire and adequate for his holy design for man's salvation. Scripture everywhere witnesses to its own inspiration. And this

> self-witness of Scripture has always had its place in the doctrine of Scripture. The doctrine does not limit its scope to a few texts about inspiration; it clearly points to the authoritative function of the written word throughout, written by men and coming to us with divine authority.[14]

Verbal inspiration

The second fact is that inspiration necessarily relates to the words. It is of God-given words that God-breathed scripture consists. It is the scriptures which are *theopneusta*; and the scriptures are the *hiera grammata* – sacred writings. There is, therefore, in inspiration a specific inner connection between the thought and the word:

> The divine superintendence which we call inspiration extended to the verbal expression of thoughts of the sacred writers, as well as to the thoughts themselves, and hence, the Bible considered as a record, an utterance of the divine revelation, is the Word of God to us.[15]

In the record the church is continuously confronted with the concrete words of God's revelation. 'The revelation is in the text itself, in the words that confront us there in all their strangeness.'[16]

This understanding of the situation is usually referred to as *verbal* inspiration. The term is used intentionally to direct attention to the result of the divine 'out-breathing' in actual words. The thought is that the Holy Spirit bore along the writers of holy scripture so that their words are to be received as in a real and decisive sense his words. If the Bible is indeed the word of God at all, it must be in such a sense that there can be no limit to which we may not trust and rely upon it to the very letter.

> Writings are made up of words, therefore there must be some form of word-inspiration. Scripture is Scripture to Christ because it has (in a way which other writing has not) God as its primary author.[17]

If words are the vehicle of thought, then, the more exact the thought the more accurate the words must be, unless they are to misrepresent and mislead. But the words of scripture do not misrepresent God's revelation nor do they mislead with regard to knowledge of him.

On three counts, however, this concept of verbal inspiration has been denied. First, because it is maintained that inspiration has to do with the person behind the record alone. 'From whence did the prophets get their inspiration?' asks H. H. Rowley. The answer he gives to his own question is that 'it was ever from their experience of God that they found their inspiration'.[18] The statement is typical of a large number of modern writers whose several declarations 'do not deal as such with a God-breathed Scripture as with inspired persons'.[19]

But the vital question to be asked is, what have we for faith? Is it inspired men in the far past, or an inspired book in the living present? Only one answer meets the need and speaks to the situation. What is needed is an inspired book in which God's revelation is made sure and contemporary.

> The God-breathed character of Scripture cannot be deduced from the piety of the biblical authors living in fellowship with God. It is related to concrete words, to the written Scriptures which are called 'God-breathed'.[20]

Akin to this restriction of inspiration to persons is the contention that it is limited to the quickened thoughts, concepts or insights of the writers alone. 'Where does inspiration lie, in the words or the total thoughts' of the biblical recorders? asks J. W. C. Wand. 'It would be probably true to say,' he replies, 'that the traditional answer would affirm the first, while our contemporary answer would be more likely to affirm the second.'[21] This would certainly be the answer given by those who take the modern view that the Bible is at most a mere human witness to the reality, or the possibility, of divine revelation. But it is nevertheless inadequate. An inspiration that is not conveyed or conveyable is of little practical use. Those who imagine that there can be inspiration of scripture which is not verbal may have some notion of divine ideas floating in the air like 'songs without words', like a crop of 'airy nothings'. But what turns them to shape and gives them local habitation and a name are the words.

When a person says something he expresses himself; and the medium of this self-expression is language. So, as James Orr says,

> Thought of necessity takes shape and is expressed in words. If there is inspiration at all, it must penetrate words as well as thought, must mould the expression, and make the language employ the living medium of the idea to be conveyed.[22]

It is not said that holy men thought as they were moved by the Holy Spirit, but that they spake. Not simply were their ideas God-inspired, but their verbal expression was under the control of the same Spirit. Inspired thought there may be, but it has no permanent significance unless it is finalized in words and thus made capable of adequate transmission. Since the Bible is the word of God, it is consequently a divinely determined record, 'not in words which man's wisdom teacheth, but in words which the Holy Spirit teacheth' (1 Corinthians 2:13). That is precisely why scripture itself directs us to its words. Never does it call attention to mere thoughts, or state that any single utterance is the writer's own idea or insight. The record is in a 'form of sound words'; words which in their fullest and final reading mediate Christ, and so are 'spirit and life' (John 6:63).

In the third place we must note the constant rejection among modern writers of verbal inspiration following from the easy equation of it with a 'mechanical', 'materialistic', or 'dictational' process, in which the human agents are conceived as passive instruments in God's hands. It is, in fact, not unusual then to designate verbal inspiration so understood as 'fundamentalist', and thus *ipso facto* 'obscurantist', and 'out of date'.

But it is this simple identification of verbal inspiration with one or other of these terms which is at fault, for no discriminating advocate of verbal inspiration conceives of it as a dictation by God on passive instruments. The idea that the human authors of scripture were so many typewriters on which the Spirit of God hammered out the words of scripture is as untenable as the opposite error which sees nothing more in inspiration than ideas derived from human insight. There is not in divine inspiration the least suppression of human individuality. It is rather that the divine moulds the human to its ends; the result is that God's strength is made perfect in man's weakness. The treasures of God are thus made available in earthen vessels. 'The divine authorship,' says Karl Rahner, 'neither competes with, nor derogates from, the human authorship; the latter is not diminished, it is not reduced to a mere secretarial function.'[23]

Warfield speaks of the method of revelation and inspiration as a 'concursive operation', one nevertheless in which the Holy Spirit is not conceived of as standing outside the human powers, ready merely to supplement any inadequacies. Rather, the divine Spirit is seen to be working confluently in, with, and by, the human authors, and thereby, elevating, directing, controlling, and energizing them as his instruments. In this way do they sometimes rise above themselves, do his work, reach his aim. To speak, then, about verbal inspiration is to emphasize the result of this action of the Spirit in words; it is not to specify the method. In the last analysis, indeed, the precise nature of inspiration cannot be given exact statement. The process is God's secret; a miracle of God, and as such has no 'explanation' outside himself. The scriptures are for us absolute because they are the speech of God, intelligible because they are in the language of man.

So long as the phrase *verbal inspiration* is given its proper connotation it should be retained. It makes clear that the inspiration of scripture is not a natural process, but the act of the Spirit of God. Nor yet is it a partial process – not a part of the Bible, but the Bible in all its parts constitutes God's written word.

Men of faith will not consider it a thing impossible with God, who is Lord of all life, for the fulfilment of his plan of grace, to deal with chosen men for the sake of humanity. 'To enlarge or inform any faculty is evidently a secondary operation of the same power by which it was first given and quickened.'[24] This does not mean that the human faculties of the selected messengers do not act according to their natural laws even though they were supernaturally strengthened. The man is not converted into a machine, even in the hands of God. In that required union of the divine and the human the message of God is given. But to be complete the message must find its fulfilment in language. Without it the mysteries unveiled before the eyes of the seer would remain confused shadows; with it they become permanent and authoritative for human life. When addressed to man, the human element becomes a part of the divine message, since the divine message can be grasped only when defined and moulded according to the laws of man's own nature. This means, emphatically, that the book is rightly said to be inspired no less than the prophet.

The book will, of course, reflect and perpetuate the peculiar idiosyncrasies of each prophet, but it will not create them. The prophet is not merely a man who sees, he is one who speaks what he sees: he is, in a profound sense, a speaking man. In the scriptures we have not just what the prophet or the apostle thought, we have the declarative and convictive language of what was given to him from above. Unless this is so there is an end of all certainty. The writing does not introduce any limitation into the representation. For man the purely spiritual is but a vague thing – a dream, perchance. It is language which is the condition of his being, the determining factor and the essential medium of ideas which are divine in origin. In the process of biblical inspiration, then, are combined harmoniously the two factors, the divine ideas and the human language. Each element performs its own specific work, and in the union the letter becomes as perfect as the spirit. And this combination of the divine and the human reflected in the scriptures has its clearest archetype in the Incarnation, in which is exhibited the divine and the human in highest form as the Word made flesh.

What 'inspiration' does not mean

Only a brief section can be given to a statement of what inspiration means negatively. The idea of the verbal inspiration of the Bible does not mean the exclusion of all non-revelatory material. It is sometimes asked, Can wrong utterances be inspired? This question arises from a confusion between revelation and inspiration. Such statements as the mistaken

views of Job's friends, the letters of the heathen kings, the lies of
Satan, the falsehoods told by Peter, were certainly not inspired
on the lips of those who made them. But the recording of these
words by the writers of scripture are the subject of the Spirit's
inspiration because needed by God for the context and perpetuation of his revelation. On this account they have been faithfully and accurately preserved.

Neither does the idea of inspiration mean that the Bible is
totally preserved from textual corruption. God never works
magically, although he does act miraculously. He has seen fit to
put his revelation in the form of written speech – in a book – but
he has not seen fit to exempt it from the normal processes which
befall human means of transmission. Books burn; and from the
fires the Bible has not been immune. Our Lord fed the multitude
miraculously by multiplying bread; but each had to eat it for
himself – and some, perhaps, with poor digestive organs. It was
not magically put within them. It did not bypass the natural
process. Immediately it is performed, any miracle wrought by
God has its natural consequences which become subject to the
normal conditions of human experience.

This, then, is the conclusion to which we are led. In stating
that the Bible is divinely inspired it is necessary to conclude that
it is verbally inspired. But to insist that it is verbally inspired is
not to specify the method of inspiration. Verbal inspiration has
nothing to do with a 'mechanical' notion. The inspiration for
which we contend has reference to the whole Bible, as it has
reference to the words themselves.

The biblical doctrine of inspiration, as the verbalization of God's
disclosure, assures that God's word is contemporary with every
age. Christians truly repose their belief on the utterances of this
book as being properly the oracles of God. The whole body of
Christian literature bears witness everywhere to it, being
everywhere vocal with the living faith in the divine trustworthiness of scripture in every one of its affirmations. This is the basis
for the frequent transition made in the Bible between God and
the scriptures. For in a fundamental sense the words of scripture
are one with the words of God.

5
THE SCRIPTURE OF TRUTH

The factuality of *truth* is all-persuasive in the biblical revelation. For that revelation presents God as the God of truth, Christ as the embodiment of truth, the divine Paraclete as the Spirit of truth, the inspired writings as the scripture of truth, and the evangelical gospel as the word of truth. From the first to last the Bible is concerned with truth. It is the only book truly honest to God, to man made in his image, and to his world. In no other book are falsehood, deceit and lying so consistently condemned (cf. e.g. Exodus 20:16). In no other book is truth of such concern. But what is the nature of the truth which the Bible so consistently affirms, contends for, and therefore requires? When Pilate raised the question of the ages, 'What is truth?' he had possibly the Greek notion of truth in view; truth to which the mind could consent, something to be thought or affirmed. Truth thus conceived has mainly to do with an actual state of affairs in contrast with what is false or fictitious. So a particular affirmation is said to be true if it corresponds to sure facts or is consistent with the laws of sound reasoning.

Reliability

This idea is certainly present in the biblical words for truth, but even more fundamental here is the thought of stability, firmness, reliability. Added therefore to the intellectual concept of truth in the Bible there is this basic moral connotation. An illustration of this moral sense of truth, with its personal and existential interactions, comes in Joseph's justification for the imprisonment of his brethren. You are being detained, he tells them, 'that your words may be tested, whether there is truth in you' (Genesis 42:16). Joseph sought to prove whether their speech corresponded to the fact, whether they were truly dependable and consistent. It is for this reason that the Hebrew word *'emet* rendered 'truth' in the AV, is frequently rendered 'faithfulness' in the RSV (cf. e.g. Deuteronomy 32:4; Psalm 108:4; 146:6; Hosea 2:20). So God as true is absolutely faithful. His truth ('faithfulness') reaches to the clouds (Psalm 108:4) and endures forever (Psalm 117:2). This absolute faithfulness of God consequently assures his complete trustworthiness; it is grounded in his own being. For all God says and does is consistent with his divine nature. God is, then, the God of truth (Deuteronomy 32:4; Psalm 31:5; 146:6). To his own self he must be true.

This truthfulness of God passes over as an attribute of what God is in himself to characterize all his activities (cf. Psalm 57:3), and specifically to his word. Thus is his word 'the word of truth', because dependable and reliable. As God is truth, so is his word truth, for it is written, 'Thy word, O God, stands fast in heaven' (Psalm 119:89). Now the whole Old Testament, as we have seen, is properly to be designated, 'the word of God'. And as 'the word of God' it is absolutely 'the scripture of truth' (cf. Daniel 10:21, AV). It partakes of God's own character, of the fundamental truthfulness of him who declares, 'God is not man that he should lie' (Numbers 23:19; cf. 1 Samuel 15:29; Psalm 89:35). There can be no escaping the conclusion that the Old Testament is stamped with the character of God as divinely true. Psalm 31:5 declares that the Lord is the 'God of truth' (AV), while Psalm 119:160 affirms his word as being 'the word of truth' (cf. Psalm 19:9; 1 Kings 17:24). And in both places the same Hebrew word occurs. The same 'truth' is predicated alike of God and of his word.

The New Testament word for truth, *aletheia*, which is used in the Septuagint version (a Greek translation of the Old Testament) to translate the two Hebrew terms *'emet* and *'muna*, has the same fundamental meaning of genuineness or reality, as opposed to what is feigned, fictitious, or false. So God is said to be both 'true' (1 John 5:20; cf. John 3:33; 7:28; 8:26;

17:3; 1 Thessalonians 1:9) and 'truthful' (Romans 3:7; cf. verse 4; 15:8, etc.). And this very truth of God found incarnate reality in Christ the Lord. As such, he bears witness to the truth of God (John 8:14; cf. 18:37), and is himself God's truth (John 14:6; Ephesians 4:21; 1 John 1:14, 17). For in him the truth as absolute divine reality was given full embodiment (John 1:14) and stands in contrast with all that is seeming and unreal. And the Holy Spirit is among men and within the church as 'the Spirit of Truth' (John 14:17; 15:26; 16:13; cf. 1 John 5:7). God – Father, Son, and Spirit – is thus predicated with the character and action of truth.

Therefore it is significant how in the Epistle to the Hebrews, for example, each person of the divine triunity is associated with the Old Testament word of prophecy which finds its fulfilment in the Christ of the gospel. In Hebrews 1:5 there is a long quotation from Psalm 2 directly attributed to God, who asks the Father's question, 'For of what angel did God ever say, "Thou art my Son, today I have begotten thee?"' (cf. 8:8). In 2:11, where the context makes clear that it is Christ the Son who is not ashamed to call the 'many sons' his brethren, there follows a quotation attesting this relationship from Psalm 22 (cf. Isaiah 8:17, 18). And in 3:7f. there is a long quotation from Psalm 95 attributed directly to the Holy Spirit. Thus is the New Testament gospel, which fulfils and fills full the Old Testament, God's gospel (Romans 1:1; cf. Acts 20:24; Romans 15:16; 1 Thessalonians 2:2, 8; 1 Timothy 1:11; 1 Peter 4:17) and Christ's (Mark 1:1; Romans 1:16; 15:19; 1 Corinthians 9:12, 18; 2 Corinthians 2:12; 4:4; 9:13; 10:14, etc.). Such is the good news revealed to the holy apostles and prophets of the New Testament by the Spirit (Ephesians 3:5; cf. 1 Corinthians 2:10), for none can comprehend God's thoughts except the Spirit (1 Corinthians 2:11). It was by the Holy Spirit that the command was given to preach this gospel to the world (Acts 1:2), and in the power of the same Spirit it was proclaimed with saving effect (cf. Acts 10:38; 1 Thessalonians 1:5; cf. 2 Corinthians 6:6, 7). By the Spirit's action that same gospel of God was given permanency as divine scripture. So is the New Testament alongside the Old, 'the word of God'. It carries the signature, the 'imprimatur', of the triune God – Father, Son, and

Holy Spirit. It is thus as the gospel of our salvation the very 'word of truth' (2 Corinthians 6:7; cf. John 17:17; Galatians 2:5; Colossians 1:5; James 1:18). So is 'the truth of the gospel' (Galatians 2:5) one and the same with 'the truth of God' (Romans 3:7).

To say that the Bible is absolutely trustworthy and dependable because stamped with God's character is at one with saying that it is a book of divine truth. Since the God of truth is its ultimate author it must inevitably reflect what he is. For as God *is*, so is his word, since, as Gabriel Marcel observes, 'between being and the word there does exist an irrefragable unity'. In God the 'I am' and the 'I utter' are one and the same. As God's word, then, the Bible embodies the truth of God – truthfully. In the things it discloses concerning God in his relation to the world and man it does not deceive, and in all it teaches it is neither misleading nor uncertain. It is right, therefore, to pronounce the holy scripture, in the words of the Westminster Catechism of 1647, 'infallible truth'. Although written by fallible men, the Bible nevertheless enshrines the self-revelation of the only true God and Jesus Christ whom he has sent (John 17:3).

Infallibility

The reality of inspiration is the guarantee of the Bible's infallibility. These two – inspiration and infallibility – go together. They are, in fact, like the reverse sides of the same coin. A God-inspired book is a divinely infallible scripture. It is arbitrary sharply to distinguish between the two ideas so as to suggest, as has been done of late, that it is possible to accept the Bible as inspired, and yet hesitate to declare it infallible. We cannot believe that there is any imperfection in God, and we dare not impute to his word any lack of truthfulness.

When, however, we say that the scripture is a book of infallible truth we are not suggesting that it is a sort of general knowledge encyclopaedia with ready-made answers to every question under the sun. The Bible is concerned with a special type of knowledge

– with 'saving truth'. Biblical knowledge is theological knowledge, and 'theology is about man and God, about God as the creator and saviour of man'.[1] It is the purpose of scripture 'to instruct for salvation' (cf. 1 Timothy 3:15f.). The Bible is, then, infallible as God's saving revelation. This fact does not, however, allow the conclusion that the trustworthiness of the Bible relates merely to 'spiritual' truth, that its statements on other matters are not necessarily accurate, that, while its message is to be accepted as reliable, the events in which that message purports to be enshrined are not. Such a disjunction between the natural and the spiritual is to be rejected. For God's word came in the context of events in the spatial-temporal world over which he is Lord. And the revelatory meaning is known only in relation to these events. It is impossible to pronounce on where 'faith' ends and the historical details begin. Nor is it finally for us to say what is, and what is not, a matter of faith. To contend for scripture as infallible truth is to contend for it in its totality as an inspired volume. To use the term 'infallibility' of the Bible is to declare that it possesses 'an indefectible authority'.[2]

In the early age of the church, and consequent upon the rediscovery of the 'word of God' at the Reformation, the Bible was accepted without question in the Christian community as infallible truth because divinely inspired. Beginning in the immediate post-Darwinian period, however, for a number of reasons, loss of faith in the absolute trustworthiness of the biblical record became widespread in the church. The basic cause for this shift away from the historical position was the virtual abandonment by the new school of critical scholars of the traditional doctrine of verbal inspiration. 'The rise of biblical scholarship made necessary a new doctrine of the inspiration of Holy Scripture,' declares Alan Richardson.[3] This necessity arose, Richardson adds, because it was found 'clearly impossible to continue to hold to the old "dictation" theory'.[4] It became the habit among liberal-minded writers to pillorize verbal inspiration as 'dictational', 'literal', or 'mechanical', and thereupon to reject it out of hand. The real purpose was to provide an excuse to exempt the words of scripture from the process of inspiration, and so allow for a radical application of the critical method. The idea was then made popular that it was not the Bible itself but the men only behind it who were in some way the subjects of the Spirit's inspiration. But the 'possession' granted these human authors of scripture did not much affect the humanness of their productions; and it certainly was not of a kind to keep the Bible free, as Burnaby asserts, of 'inconsistencies and contradictions, not only on points of historical fact, but in matters of "faith and morals"'.[5] The result of this weakened conception of inspiration, Marcus Dods admitted, although not himself an advocate of verbal inspiration, was to undermine biblical infallibility.[6] Driver had earlier scorned the very idea of a verbally inspired Bible and asserted that whatever inspiration the writers of the Bible possessed it certainly did not assure their freedom from 'imperfection, error, and mistake in matters of fact'.[7]

Charles Gore did much to induce those disposed to accept the verdicts of criticism as assured results to settle for a fallible Bible. He believed that the time was long past when Christian faith could be tied to an infallible scripture. He deplored any attempt to renew trust in the authenticity and accuracy of the biblical record. He was disturbed because he thought he saw signs of a revival 'of the position that faith in Christianity, as really the divinely-given gospel for the world, is bound up with the old-fashioned belief in the Bible as an infallible book'.[8] And without the least inhibition he declares that the Bible is not without its mistakes and that its authors used traditions and folklore as if they were factually true. Such statements are typical of those who espoused the critical cause. Even the most spiritually sensitive and evangelically sympathetic among them continued to insist that whatever part the Holy Spirit played in the process of inspiration it did not result in giving us a scripture of infallible truth.

Thus H. H. Rowley, far from treating the scriptures sceptically, nevertheless contends that divine inspiration came through the personality of men signally consecrated to God and sensitive to his Spirit, but who yet were men of limited outlook who approached their task from false presuppositions.[9] It is in their own experience of God that their inspiration is to be found.[10] He declares that were the human authors of the Old Testament 'helpless instruments in the hands of God, completely controlled by Him, the revelation would be independent of their personality, but if they were imperfect and fallible, then their imperfections and fallibilities could not but affect the revelation'.[11] His conclusion is that the Old Testament does not give an exact record of history, true in detail, or even authoritative revelations of the future, or yet wholly trustworthy self-disclosures of God. It is rather a record of men who reached out after God and responded to God's reaching after them. Rowley believes that the New Testament follows a like pattern. The idea of inspiration is fundamentally the same as in the former Testament. There is no verbal infallibility; indeed, there are here, too, inaccuracies and reflections of the ideas and expectations of the fallible authors. The case of the New Testament is as that of the Old; each of its writers was, as Paul, 'charged with a divinely given message, but for the form in which it was delivered he was himself responsible. He was the ambassador, not the postman'.[12] We could go on and on with statements of similar content and intent from writer after writer, but it seems pointless to do so. For there is a fundamental agreement among them all that whatever is meant by inspiration, the Bible is not verbally inspired, and whatever authority it may possess it is not that of infallible truth.

All who begin with the presupposition that the Bible is a patchwork affair, the fallible production of men however strangely warmed in spirit by their overwhelming sense of the divine, and to whom the critical method is omnipotent, are bound to come up with the same conclusion regarding the Bible. In saying this we do not suggest that it is not legitimate to approach the Bible in a scientific manner. Of course it must be the subject of the most careful and searching scrutiny. As Leon Morris forcefully puts it: 'We should not take the books of the Bible out of the realm of literature generally and put them in a glass case where no awkward questions can be asked and take no notice of genre, individual peculiarities and the like. But we should not forget either that God has spoken through these writings. We do them less than justice if we treat them as though we were atheists or agnostics.'[13] Criticism must be allowed to discover for us what it can of the circumstances and composition of scripture. But it must not be allowed to rob us of God by draining out of the Bible what is essentially divine. True, much of modern biblical study and research is learned in the extreme, but as Morris observes, it becomes tentative and even embarrassed when it comes to hearing a word from God. For why after all should preachers or congregations pay attention to it if they do not hear therein the voice of God in truth? Any approach to the study of the Bible which prevents men from finding God through it and within it is bound to result in a loss of faith and a lack of interest in scripture.

It is indeed unfortunate 'that much of the excellent scholarly work being done in these days tends to hinder rather than help the humble men of faith'.[14] We go back, then, to insist on the position stated in the earlier part of this chapter that the Bible as the word of God partakes of the truth of which God is. His word is truth. And God's truth is – must be – infallible truth.

Yet the affirmation of faith in the Bible as the infallible truth, some think, needs to be strengthened by a declaration of its inerrancy. Infallibility relates to truth; inerrancy relates to facts. So a distinction may be drawn which permits some to affirm that while the biblical facts may not be as they are presented, yet there is truth conveyed by them and such truth is infallible. But the question must be asked: since truth is the interpretation of facts, must not the facts be as they are, if the truth is to be as it is? If the writers are erroneous as to the facts, can their interpretation be infallible as to truth?

Inerrancy

Such questions launch us into a discussion of the subject of inerrancy which has become again focal in recent debate. Yet the word itself, and what it intends to guarantee regarding the Bible, has a long history. Somewhere during the last quarter of the nineteenth century the controversy over the inerrancy of scripture broke out in earnest. Writing in 1894, A. J. Gordon refers to 'inerrancy of scripture' as a 'modern phrase'.[15] Previous to that, A. B. Bruce, in association with three American scholars, C. A. Briggs, L. J. Evans, and H. P. Smith, had produced their volume entitled, *Inspiration and Inerrancy* (1891) in which, under the influence of the new critical method, they declared openly and unequivocally against the later concept of the title. But for the most part, the great evangelical biblical scholars and preachers, Liddon, Parker, Spurgeon, Moule, Ryle, to name a few, maintained the inerrancy of biblical facts and the infallibility of the biblical truth. J. C. Ryle, looking back to the Christian leaders of the previous century, Grimshaw, Venn, Berridge, and others, says, 'They never flinched from asserting that there can be *no error* in the Word of God.'[16] John Wesley was equally emphatic; writing in his *Journal* for Wednesday, July 24 1776, he says, 'If there be any mistakes in the Bible, there may well be a thousand. If there be one falsehood in that book, it did not come from the God of truth.' Wesley's affirmation of the Bible's inerrancy is but a re-echo of that of Augustine. 'I do most firmly affirm,' declares the North African bishop, regarding the 'scriptural books', 'that no one of these authors has erred in any respect in writing.'[17] The truth of the matter is that, as Clark Pinnock declares,

> Inerrancy is to be regarded as an essential concomitant of the doctrine of inspiration, a necessary inference drawn from the fact that Scripture is God's Word.[18]

It was not, as we have made clear elsewhere, until the rise of the deistic rationalism of the early eighteenth century that its absolute truthfulness was called in question. So James Packer is not going beyond the facts in declaring that 'evangelicals are accustomed to speak of the Word of God as *infallible* and *inerrant*'.[19]

The best way to proceed in considering the issue of biblical inerrancy is to follow the reasoning and reckoning of one of its specific opponents. In this connection A. G. Hebert is typical and most vigorous. He makes an attack on those whom he refers to as 'fundamentalists',[20] who, he declares, in holding to 'verbal inspiration', are guilty of advocating a 'materialistic conception of inspiration'.[21] They boldly, and in Hebert's estimation, blindly, assert that the Bible is 'free from error' and therefore 'inerrant'. He thereupon adduces a number of 'duplicate' and 'inconsistent' accounts designed to show that the 'doctrine of the Inerrancy of the Bible must be regarded as, at least in reference to material fact, extremely vulnerable'.[22] Using the designation 'fundamentalist', apparently with opprobrious intent, he goes on, quite against the evidence, to assert that no previous age had ever regarded scripture without fault in the manner of 'literal inerrancy' as it is now being proclaimed.[23] Theological and religious inerrancy was the most, he contends, that those of other times affirmed. But the 'materialistic inerrancy' now being advocated, he charges, 'has been a potent cause of modern unbelief'.[24]

Having stated his position thus forcefully, Hebert proceeds to attack the Inter-Varsity Fellowship of Christian Unions in general, and *The New Bible Commentary* in particular, for favouring inerrancy. Both words 'infallibility' and 'inerrancy', he points out, are negative, and are therefore, he judges, 'troublesome and unsatisfactory'. So he pronounces the 'rigid theory of factual inerrancy' to be 'too narrow'.[25] Considering the Old Testament by itself, Hebert's verdict is that it contains errors, 'not in small matters of literal fact, but in matters of faith and morals'.[26] He admits it is a 'paradox' to assert 'the Book of God's Truth' contains 'error'. But 'a deeper consideration of the words "truth" and "error" will solve the problem since,' he assures us, 'the "error" is not of the absolute sort'.[27]

It is certainly extraordinary to assert, in one and the same breath, that 'the Book of God's Truth' contains error, not in small matters of literal fact, but in matters of faith and morals, and that its 'errors' are not of an absolute sort.

Errors in faith and morals is surely a serious matter. And it is truly more than a paradox to affirm that God's truth is not fully true. It seems that Hebert gives no consistent meaning of the terms 'truth' and 'error'. In fact, it may well be the case that his very equivocations show up the need for such a word as 'inerrancy' in our day to safeguard the fact that God's truth is not less than true, as *homoousios* ('of the same substance' with the Father) was required at the time of Athanasius to secure the fact that our Lord does not possess less than full Godhood.

In some quarters today exception is taken to the application of the term inerrancy to the scriptures on the score that, although it is not strewn with inconsistencies and errors as liberal critical scholars seem sometimes to suggest, it has nevertheless a limited number of factual mistakes which just cannot be explained away. Is the issue then just a matter of statistics? Can we speak of the Bible as infallible truth if it has, whatever the number – is it ten errors? – but not be designated infallible, except in some ambiguous sense, if it goes beyond that number? It is rather more in accord with the way of things that 'once granted that there is error it is possible to go far and fast'. For if 'the Bible keeps making mistakes in matters scientific the suspicion arises that this flaw in the background is going to distort the foreground'.[28] The history of biblical studies has indeed made it 'apparent that scholars who abandoned the trustworthiness of Biblical history had furnished an entering edge for the abandonment of doctrinal elements. Theoretically such an outcome might perhaps have been avoided by an act of will, but in practice it was not.'[29]

If the Bible gives us the revelation of God's truth it does seem difficult to accept that it can be in error regarding the basic events in which that revelation was enshrined. More acceptable to the needs of the situation is Geoffrey Bromiley's statement in the *New Bible Commentary*:

> While it is no doubt a paradox that eternal truth is revealed in temporal events and witnessed through a human book, it is sheer unreason to say that truth is revealed in and through that which is erroneous.[30]

In sum, then, the argument of this chapter is that the Bible contains infallible and inerrant truth. As infallible it possesses the quality of never deceiving or misleading, and so is 'wholly trustworthy and reliable'; as 'inerrant', it is 'wholly true'. Scripture is termed infallible and inerrant to express the conviction that all its teaching is the utterance of God 'who cannot lie', whose word, once spoken, abides for ever, and that therefore it may be trusted implicitly.[31]

Yet it must be acknowledged that nowhere does the Bible claim inerrancy for itself in actual terms. But so constant throughout is its reference to truth, and so numerous the declarations of 'thus saith the Lord', that the whole record seems to be covered by the one all-comprehensive phrase, the word of God. And God's word is a true word, an infallible and an inerrant word. Maybe both words, as Packer allows, 'are not essential for stating the evangelical view'.[32] It is a fact, nevertheless, which scripture itself makes evident, that the tie between God and scripture is an absolute and vital tie. And even if some, often because of a failure to understand its significance and cogency, fight shy more especially of the word inerrancy, the truth which the term intends must follow from a right view of divine inspiration. For the fact that the human authors were under the control of the Spirit must mean that they were kept faithful in committing God's revelation to writing. While the terms inerrant and infallible are not themselves biblical, 'yet they do, nonetheless, express a crucial aspect of the doctrine of inspiration; namely, that the Bible is wholly trustworthy and wholly true'.[33] The biblical doctrine of revelation carries with it the assurance that in all its parts it is infallible as to its truth and inerrant as to its facts. The case is in the last issue, as J. W. Montgomery states: 'The doctrine of biblical inerrancy derives from the attitude of Scripture towards itself, and in particular the attitude of Christ towards Scripture.'[34]

Two final comments need to be made in bringing this chapter to its close. It has been general in doctrinal statements to refer divine inspiration to the scripture, 'as originally given'. But we do not possess the Bible in this form. It has not come to us directly, as it were, from its inspired authors. We know from the existence of its many manuscripts and their variant readings that its several writings are not word for word the same in each. If then we have not got the Bible 'as originally given' what becomes of the claim to its infallibility and inerrancy? The question is pressed on us, especially by those who refuse to equate the word of God with the biblical record. Thus, for example, Brunner challenges us regarding this original Bible, of which he says, 'two things only are known; first, that it was the infallible Word of God, and, second, that although it is very different from the present one, it was still the same Bible.'[35] But the dilemma is not at all as serious as Brunner supposes. The Bible as originally given is not *very different* from the Bible we now have. The very multiplicity of manuscripts shows that between the two there is remarkable agreement. The science of textual criticism assures us that we have substantially the scripture as originally given. The truth is, as R. A. Finlayson says, 'That the original is all but identical with the text we possess, the margin of difference being so small that only one text in a thousand is open to uncertainty on textual grounds, while, moreover, no doctrine of the faith is thereby involved in uncertainty.'[36]

The other matter requiring some remarks concerns the apparent discrepancies and errors which do appear to be present in the Bible despite all assertions of its infallibility and inerrancy. It is surely useless to contend that the Bible is infallible if in point of fact it is in error. No view of inspiration can be entertained which does not take account of the phenomena of scripture itself as well as its didactic statements. If indeed contradictions and errors abound in the book of God, then it is in vain to maintain that it was written under the control of the Spirit's influence which precludes all error. The issue is then one of fact. Do the authors of scripture contradict themselves or each other? Does the Bible teach as true anything which from any other source can be proved false? The question is not whether the views of a particular writer are incorrect, but whether he actually teaches what is erroneous. It is, for example, not a question whether a writer himself believed the earth was flat or square, but whether he declared it to be true that it is.

Some errors have been credited to the biblical writers which are due rather to the reader's failure to pay attention to the writer's method of recording, or to note his use of language.

Much of scripture is in the form of narrative. A true report of an event may be either a verbatim account, or a synopsis which focuses the salient points, or, in selective form so as to spotlight a specific person, theme, or group. Taking as an example the parallel passages in the gospels which sometimes show wide divergencies, E. J. Young maintains that they are quite consistent with the principle of 'inerrancy'. By 'inerrancy', he stresses, is not meant that each account should be in exactly the same words, but that each writer told the truth, recorded the matter accurately, has given us a true picture of what transpired.[37] He takes the quotations from the Old Testament in the New in the same way; they reveal that there was 'no mechanical, parrot-like repetition'.[38] The human writers acted as responsible agents; and it is precisely here, he contends, that 'we begin to understand the true nature of verbal inspiration and also inerrancy'.[39]

Although God's revelation is for all time, it came in the form it did in the language of the day. It was not the language of formal logic, or of scientific statement. Much of the biblical language is idiomatic popular, non-technical. Where such language occurs it must not be taken as strictly literal fact. When a biblical writer, for example, speaks of the four corners of the earth it is surely wrong to credit him with teaching as divine truth that the earth is square. 'Inspiration is a means to an end,' says Warfield, 'and not an end in itself; if the truth is accurately conveyed to the ear that listens to it, its full end is obtained.'[40] There is nothing either in a writer's method of recording, or in his use of language, which tells against the infallible truth and inerrant facts of the Bible.

It is not relevant to deal here with the several alleged errors chronicled by those who reject the absolute truthfulness of the Scriptures. To discuss each one would require more than one additional volume. A few observations may, however, be useful. The questions posed at the beginning of this section suggest that there are two broad types of error alleged to be found in the biblical record: contradictions and inconsistencies.

On the first of these three points may be made. (i) Some adduced contradictions will be found on further reflection to be more apparent than real. (ii) Many of them are in any case only concerned with trivial matters. (iii) In other instances statements which stand in contradiction will sometimes find their resolution in the context of fuller biblical truth. Leon Morris illustrates how this works out in reference to David's numbering of the children of Israel. In 2 Samuel 24:1, it is stated:

> The anger of the LORD was kindled against Israel, and he incited David against them saying, 'Go, number Israel and Judah.'

But in 1 Chronicles 21:1 we read, 'Satan stood up against Israel, and incited David to number Israel.' It is said that the Chronicler did not accept the theology of the passage in Samuel, and so substituted his own view. But is it not possible to accept that both passages are not finally contradictory? In so far as the numbering of Israel was an evil it had its source in the evil one. But from another point of view the hand of God was in it:

> 'It is the uniform picture in Scripture that Satan has no absolute control power. He can operate only within the limits God prescribes. But if God permits his activities there is a sense in which He is responsible. He may even be termed the author of these activities.'[41]

And does not the opening chapter of the book of Job confirm this explanation?

From time to time error has been claimed for certain biblical statements because they have been held to conflict with scientific, geological and historical facts. But all we need say on this, the second issue, here is that

(i) without going into detail, it can be asserted that some biblical declarations once held to be erroneous have been proven accurate by the findings of archaeology; while light has been thrown by the same means on passages otherwise long obscure. One example of this turnabout concerns Luke's statements in his gospel (3:1), and in Acts (13:7). For long it was claimed that he was in error in affirming that Lysanias was contemporary tetrarch with the Herodian rulers, and that the island of Cyprus was ruled by a pro-consul. But archaeology has vindicated the historical accuracy of Luke on both counts.

(ii) Sometimes it has been supposed that statements in the Bible have been in error because at odds with existing scientific knowledge only to find the particular scientific claim itself later falsified.

(iii) We must distinguish between what the Bible actually says and specific, and sometimes preconceived interpretations of it. It is well-known that the church at one time thought the Bible assured the Ptolemaic view of the universe. But now we see that it can be explained, without violence being done to its language, in the Copernican system.

(iv) Even if other difficulties cannot be resolved and all inconsistencies reconciled, it does not follow that the Bible is, therefore, other than Christian faith has from the first claimed it to be. 'I accept the universe,' said the cynical agnostic lady to Thomas Carlyle. 'Madam, you had better,' was his cryptic reply. The universe was right there as an inescapable fact which would be sheer folly to deny. But has not Bishop Butler made clear that there are apparent discrepancies in nature and inconsistencies beyond obvious reconciliation? And with these acknowledged it had still to be accepted as a hard fact. By analogy, then, it is not unreasonable to suppose that there must be some things in revelation beyond what reason can fully fathom and correlate. Or, 'Have we to wait a communication from Tübingen, or a telegram from Oxford, before we can read the Bible?'[42] Of course not. Must we then hold up belief in the Bible as God's infallible and inerrant Word until all its alleged discrepancies and inconsistencies have been fully resolved? The answer is the same.

We are not unaware that in the course of transmission, 'errors' in transcription and translation have crept into the text. But this admission in no way affects the issue. What is being insisted upon is that, as coming from God, the scripture is truly divine, therefore, absolutely trustworthy. This means simply that faith in the Bible rests upon the Bible's own witness to itself as the word of God. And to say that is only another way of saying that the scripture itself demands that it be taken as infallible as regards its truth, and inerrant as regards its facts.

Christ as the Word, the embodiment of divine truth, acts through the scriptures of truth by the urging and unction of him who is the Spirit of truth to the glory of God the Father

– that his name may be hallowed by trustful acceptance of the truth, his kingdom may come in loving obedience to the truth, and his will may be done on earth as it is in heaven through devoted service in the truth.

6

THE NEW TESTAMENT CHURCH AND ITS SCRIPTURES

No one can read the New Testament, which is essentially concerned with the Lord and the life of the Christian church in the beginning of its pilgrimage within human history, without being impressed by the sovereign place accorded to scripture in its creation and proclamation. The first church was born in an environment in which the Old Testament was accepted and acknowledged by the people of God as a divinely communicated word concerning man's salvation. For the messianic King of the new Israel, and, thus, for the new Israel of the messianic King, it was divinely natural to turn to its pages to trace the ways of God's progressive self-disclosure, which now 'in the fulness of time' had reached its climax in Christ Jesus. In the Old Testament Christ found the warrant for his messianic work, and the New Testament church the mandate for its saving message.

In the consciousness of the Lord of the church the Old Testament scriptures held a place of supremacy, so that his attitude to and use of these scriptures, especially for those committed to his lordship, is of decisive moment. How did Christ regard the Old Testament word? This is a question of extreme importance.

Jesus and the Old Testament

It is certain that Jesus' whole way in the world was moulded by the Old Testament writings. So true is this that R. V. G. Tasker can assert that

> at every vital point of our Lord's earthly ministry the Old Testament was there, in his heart if not in his hands, in his thoughts,

if not in his words, determining the course his ministry should take, and providing the only possible language for its interpretation.[1]

In 'all the scriptures' he sees in vital and vivid outline the holy task it was his to accomplish. 'Behind his actions lay the conciousness that he was doing precisely what it was foretold in Scripture that God's Servant should do.'[2] To Jesus the Old Testament was no less than the Father's word in which he everywhere heard his Father's voice. It was his view that what the scripture said about him, God said. The total impression is consequently all but inescapable that the Old Testament was for him an evident delight, disclosing to him the pattern for his own work and the power for his own living. In many and varying situations verbal quotations from the Old Testament or scraps of its phraseology came to him with a naturalness which shows how completely saturated was his mind with the scriptural word. In his battle with Satan in the desert of temptation he found the Old Testament the shield of his victory, – 'a shield, not of straw, but truly of brass,' as Calvin comments.

It must surely be evident to any reader of the Gospels that our Lord attached the highest and divinest significance to the Old Testament. Again and again he rang out the challenge, 'It is written,' and 'Have you not read?' He quotes from all parts of the Old Testament and condemns those who 'transgress the commandment of God by their tradition'. All his teaching is permeated by the Old Testament. He was well versed in its total message. 'His knowledge of the Scriptures was so intimate and profound that he was always able to interconnect from quite different passages of like manner and spirit. By meditation he penetrated the Scriptures as a *unity* rather than a compilation.'[3] The very language of the Old Testament was his native language. But it was also for him the natural, or more truly, the supernatural, channel of his expression, because it was concerned with his Father's business, which business he was concerned to fulfil.

There is no trace throughout his earthly ministry that he quoted the Old Testament as a matter of pious habit. Rather was his mind so steeped in the words and principles of Scripture that quotation and allusion sprang from his lips both naturally and appositely.[4] In contrast with the Rabbis of his day, who constantly appealed to tradition, Jesus is found frequently referring, in an exclusive way, to the Old Testament. His oft repeated formula, 'it is written,' being in the perfect tense, might properly be translated, 'it stands written,' thus implying the ever-present relevance of the original writings of the Old Testament scriptures. It follows, then, as Professor Tasker states:

> The testimony of our Lord to the Old Testament and his claim to divinity are, it would seem, more closely associated than many in our day are prepared to acknowledge.

And he urges with emphasis, that

> as Christians, we are bound to look at that unique literature primarily through the eyes of him who claimed to be the Light of the world, our Lord and Saviour Jesus Christ.[5]

But how precisely are we to read this attitude to and use of the Old Testament by Christ the Lord? In the context of the general purpose of this volume they can be given a threefold application. To begin with, Christ's attitude to and use of the Old Testament *validates its divinity.* Jesus certainly regarded the Old Testament – the same canonical scriptures which we still possess – as the book of God. What was written there was for him unequivocably the divine word. He surely believed it to be the very oracles of God. Christ in his divine person knew without doubt the truth about his Old Testament, knew that the events and words it recorded were from above. They were the deeds and speech of his Father whose glory he shared before this world's foundations first were laid.

> This concept of Jesus' relation to the Old Testament is anchored in his conviction that in him and in the events of his ministry the promises of God and the purposes of God in the Old Testament are coming to their fulfilment.[6]

For Jesus, then, the Old Testament was in the fullest and most authentic sense divinely valid scripture. And as such it cannot be broken (John 10:35), nor can the smallest part of a letter of the

Law fail (Luke 16:17); and all things written of him shall be accomplished (cf. Luke 18:31; 12:50; 22:37; John 19:28). It was for him fully God's word, his Father's word.

And Jesus' attitude to and use of the Old Testament, in the second place, *verifies its historicity*. His authority seals the factuality of the Old Testament story. Much that is dismissed today as legendary or fable he held to be actual: the Mosaic composition of the Pentateuch, the swallowing of Jonah by the great fish, the Davidic authorship of Psalm 110, to name but a few examples. Jesus consistently took the persons named (e.g. Abel, in Luke 2:5; Noah, in Matthew 24:37–39; Abraham, in John 8:56; Lot, in Luke 17:28–32, etc.), and the chronicled events (e.g. the manna, in John 6:31f; David's eating of the shewbread, in Matthew 12:3, 4, etc.) of the Old Testament to be real historical actualities. Christ's estimate of the historicity of the Old Testament cannot be lightly set aside.

> The relation of any Old Testament passage to Christ must be a historical one, for each statement was made on an occasion along the way which led from Abraham to Christ. Because it arose in a specific situation, the Old Testament passage has a historical context which must be taken into consideration, whether it has a direct effect on the interpretation of the passage or not.[7]

The force of Christ's use of and attitude to the Old Testament cannot be blunted by any form of 'accommodation' theory. According to some, Christ's declaration that 'Moses wrote of me' does not tie us to the Mosaic authorship of the record; nor does the reference to Jonah's three days' sojourn amid the intestines of a monster of the deep authenticate the story as 'simple history'. In his allusion to Psalm 110, Christ, it is said, was simply accepting uncritically Jewish tradition regarding Old Testament authorship, without giving it the support of an infallible guarantee. He never intended in any instance to pronounce on critical questions, nor to 'anticipate the results of scientific inquiry or historical research'.[8]

But we must ask: can it be seriously maintained that if Jesus were aware that the Jews were wrong in their view of the origin and history of their scripture, he could have 'adapted' himself to their ignorance and prejudices regarding them, when, in fact, he had come to dispel error, and even condemned those who put such store by the traditions of the elders? It does not seem right to credit him, who came as the truth, with unreadiness, on any pretext, to correct a known falsehood. In other respects he did not show himself reluctant to overthrow current erroneous beliefs. He denounced pharisaic traditionalism; he repudiated popular nationalistic expectations of messiahship, and so forth, without the least inhibition.

> Surely he would have been prepared to explain clearly the mingling of divine truth and human error in the Bible if such he had known to exist. The notion that our Lord was fully aware that the view of Holy Scripture current in his day was erroneous, and he deliberately accommodated his teaching to the beliefs of his hearers, will not square with the facts.[9]

That he should allow popular fallacies to continue must certainly seem inconsistent with the note of absolute sincerity which runs so conspicuously through all his teaching. If, as some 'accommodationists' urge, it is a harmless thing to allow that he accepted uncritically the Mosaic authorship of the Pentateuch, or the Davidic authorship of Psalm 110, then, the question must be posed, why consequently all the fuss about the results of criticism? For it is a presupposition of the critical analysis of scripture that the key to its true interpretation lies in giving the correct dating, authoring, and sectionalizing of its contents. How, then, can it be supposed that Christ interpreted them aright if he did not openly set them in the context demanded by the new analysis and the historical method?

Kenosis

Neither can the attitude to and use of the Old Testament by Jesus as verifying its historicity be disallowed by the appeal to any 'kenotic' theory. Some declare that in becoming flesh the Lord of glory so emptied himself – 'of all but love' – that during his earthly life his knowledge was vastly restricted. It is then concluded that while in general his utterances are stamped with divine truthfulness, on other issues regarded as peripheral to the fulfilment of his messianic calling he had, like the rest of us, to cope with difficulties and uncertainties. He consequently sought in the Old Testament those spiritual truths significant for his own life and that of others. But as far as the authorship and historical sequence of those writings were concerned these were questions which he did not bother to investigate, since they had no relevance in comparison with the message drawn from them. R. L. Ottley in his famous Bampton lectures of 1896 gave to this view a scholarly impress. Insisting that Christ's knowledge was limited by the conditions of incarnation, he yet allows that Christ neither deceived nor could deceive others. He insists, however, that Christ did not teach positively on all subjects he incidentally touched upon:

> It is admitted that he never teaches positively on points of science; analogy makes it equally probable that he never taught as to the authorship of different books of Scripture or their mode of composition.[10]

Of course he really could not have done so, because there is nothing to suggest that he possessed 'modern critical knowledge', or indeed 'that he intended to endorse the traditional views of his countrymen in regard to the nature of their Scriptures'.[11]

But were not these scriptures his scriptures too? Is it not then more credible to believe that he would want to know the certainty of their origin? For what if the Father had not spoken his word concerning him to the prophet to whom it is credited? He surely knew that his reference to the scriptures which spoke of him would be taken as decisive by his followers. The Jews certainly believed their scripture to be God's word because of its essential authenticity. It was for them both infallible and authoritative because its statements about its own origin were held to be trustworthy.

> Our Lord Jesus Christ endorsed this view of the Jews and made frequent use of the Old Testament as authoritative and infallible. He passed on this view, charged with his own divine authority, to the apostles and through them to the Christian church.[12]

A 'kenotic' christology which discounts Christ's supremacy as a teacher of divine truth cannot be accepted. It would present us with one less informed about the shaping of his own sacred literature, and the true religious history of his own people, as the chosen of his Father, than any callow theological student of these days. If the interpretation of Philippians 2:1–10 means that our Lord was so emptied of the knowledge he once possessed that he taught his disciples to receive as genuine and authoritative scriptures which were in fact neither, then there is an end of all certainty. From his assertion that Moses wrote of him, and that David spoke of one who would sit at God's right hand, and that Jonah was three days entombed within the walls of a fish's belly, Jesus deduced doctrines of eternal moment. But what if Moses did not write, if David did not speak so, if Jonah did not reside in a fish, can then such deductions be accepted with any confidence? Jesus looked to the Old Testament as assuring the warrant and credentials of his mission, but what follows if they were nothing of the kind? Of a book which concerned his own life and work, 'Here, if anywhere, we should expect our Lord to speak with divine authority and absolute truth.'[13]

The 'kenotic' principle as here interpreted becomes all the more disconcerting when applied to Christ's own words and teaching. Can the same assumption be referred, for example, to his stupendous claim of Matthew 11:25–28? 'No man knows the Son except the Father, and no man knows the Father except the Son' (verse 27). But what if here, too, he did not know? What if this were but a pious guess? Christ was, of course, a real man. There is nothing 'docetic' about the figure of the gospels. But he was also, what none of us is, a perfect man, supremely endowed by the Holy Spirit in the days of his flesh. Is it right, then, even on this basis, to attribute to him ignorance about the Old Testament which would inevitably be perpetuated in the New Testament church? His words were not his; they were given from the Father. Are such claims as these the assertions of pseudo-knowledge or the musings of one hedged in by the notions of his times? If, when he spoke such words, he spoke what he knew and what was true, why, except in the interests of a theory, should it be denied that his verdict on scripture was also authentic and final? He has stamped scripture with his own divine status, and in so doing he has verified its historicity.

The stamp of approval

The third significance in Jesus' attitude to and use of the Old Testament is to *validate its authority*. We have something more to say on this subject in our next chapter. It is enough here to declare with Pierre Marcel that Christ 'seals with his authority numerous facts which are related in Scripture, and the historicity of numerous events: we are therefore instructed to believe them all'.[14] For Jesus himself the Old Testament spoke as the living voice of God. And regarding it so, Christ 'has set his seal to that sacred code which ages treasured as presenting the mind of God to man. Therefore alike the Sacred Scriptures and he who is the Subject of its message are called the Word of God.'[15] As students of the Christian gospel, we see 'the most impressive characteristic of the Holy Scriptures in the fact of the attitude taken towards them by Jesus Christ'.[16] We cannot escape the New Testament stress on the absoluteness of our Lord's knowledge, and it must be applied with equal seriousness to his attitude to the use of the Old Testament. So must it be concluded with James Orr that

> so long as Christ, in his self-attesting power, commands the allegiance of believing hearts, the Bible, which contains the priceless treasure of God's Word regarding him, will remain in undiminished honour. It will be read, prized, and studied by devout minds, while the world lasts.[17]

This Old Testament which Jesus esteemed as divinely authentic was the Bible which the apostles and preachers of the gospel of the first days of the church took with them as they went about declaring that Messiah had come and that Jesus is Lord. They found in the Old Testament a clear witness to the Christ whose divinity it attested and way of salvation it prefigured. For these evangelists of the good news

> the Old Testament, as a whole and in all its parts, was a witness to Christ. It was God's word written, to be studied with heart and

mind, both as a comprehensive unity and in its minutest particulars. This earliest Christian view of Scripture derives from and underlies the view of Scripture taught by our Lord. In the New Testament Christ's view is the Christian view of Scripture.[18]

In their regard for the Old Testament the apostolic men knew themselves to be following Christ's clear example. They believed, as R. T. France states, that

> to his coming the whole Old Testament had looked forward; not only the actual predictions of the prophets and the psalms, but the very pattern of God's working recorded in the Old Testament was preparing for the final and perfect work of God, which in his coming had begun. In him we move from shadows to reality; in him God's purposes are fulfilled at last, and all that now remains is the working out of this fulfilment to its final consummation. Thus Jesus' use of the Old Testament falls into a single coherent scheme, with himself at the focus.[19]

For this regard for the Old Testament these apostolic men knew themselves to be following Christ's clear example. And they felt as by a divinely-inspired instinct, as G. A. Smith says, 'What was indispensable to the Redeemer must be always indispensable to the redeemed.'

The relation between the Testaments

It will not, therefore, come as any surprise to find the New Testament saturated with the Old. For the one fact stands out that 'The New Testament's proclamation is founded on the Old Testament.'[20] It is nevertheless very difficult to give an exact total of the number of references made by the New Testament writers to the former Testament because their thought is suffused by its message and articulates its words.

Horne has computed that there are about 263 direct quotations from the Old in the New. Others give higher figures. A conservative estimate is that there are some 352 verses of the New Testament made up of direct quotations from the Old. If clear allusions are added, the list is much greater. C. H. Toy lists 613 such instances; Dittmar 1,640; while Eugen Huchn states that there are 4,105 passages in the whole New Testament reminiscent of the Old Testament scriptures.

Shire classifies the literary parallels between the two Testaments under four major headings. Subsumed under class one are those prefaced by a formula of introduction such as 'God said', or 'it is written', or as 'spoken by' such and such a prophet. Of these Shire reckons the number is 239. Class two is made up of 198 Old Testament quotations without introduction or acknowledgement. The third class consists of New Testament verses in which the Old Testament material has been distinctly utilized, and constitutes the large total of 1,167 instances. Class four has to do with indirect or probable dependence upon the Old Testament, but Shire does not give any numeration here. The impressive total of the first three classes shows 1,604 New Testament passages in the New Testament directly dependent on the Old Testament.[21]

The New Testament heralds of the Christian gospel certainly did not abandon their Old Testament. They accepted it, as did their Lord, as to its divinity, historicity, and authority. They found Christ in their Old Testament. So true is this that Paul at times 'seems to think of Christ as the speaker or else spoken to in various Old Testament passages'.[22] Specially illuminating, indeed, is Paul's use of the Old Testament. It was for him the divine and progressive unveiling of God's purpose of redemption which climaxed in Christ the Lord. Thus his 'devotion to the Scripture was not that of a Rabbi; he did not cite the Scripture from a sense of duty or a love of theology or tradition, but because of their witness to Christ.'[23] Yet he saw in the Old Testament a word with which to silence all objections; for him its every part was prefaced, either openly or by implication, with 'thus says the Lord'. In their attitude to and use of the Old Testament Paul and the other New Testament writers sometimes go as far as to base their whole argument upon a single passage of scripture. And the fact that 'it is written' clinched a truth (cf. Acts 23:5; Romans 4:3, 9; 15:9–11; 1 Corinthians 6:16; Galatians 3:8, 10, 13; Hebrews 1:2, 2:12, etc.). In Galatians 3:16 Paul rests his case on the grammatical form of a single word.

It must seem, then, to be inescapable that the New Testament writers did not feel themselves free to pick and choose what they wished from their Old Testament. For the 'correspondence in the use and interpretation of the Old Testament is an especially significant aspect of the unified message of the early church'.[24] The Sadducees of our Lord's time rejected parts of the revealed word: the Pharisees, on the other hand, added to it their rubrics and rituals. Both came under the stinging rebuke of Christ. In no place do we find the apostles ever doubting or challenging the divinity, historicity, or authority of any scriptural utterance or event.

In the process of time the New Testament took its place alongside the Old Testament as the scriptures of the church. Christ came among men as the incarnate Word, the very Voice of God expressed in terms of human existence. He proclaimed, as himself the divine Word and messianic King, the message of God's kingdom, and the presence among men of God's promised salvation. His words, he asserted, were the Father's words, his acts the Father's acts.

The early church

The first preachers of the gospel were sure that they had this Word of God in and through Christ, and that they had been entrusted with a divinely communicated message. The gospel word was, of course, at the beginning orally given. It was in this sense a 'tradition'. The word 'tradition' means literally 'that which is handed over'. Thus was gospel message something handed over, and to be passed on. Against the rabbinical traditions given the same reverent status by the Jewish ecclesiastics as the word of God, Jesus took a firm stand (cf. Mark 7:3f.). But the New Testament writers use the term for the deposit of teaching given to his apostolic men by Jesus himself before and after his resurrection (cf. 2 Thessalonians 2:15; cf. 3:6). This was for them the true tradition which was not 'of man', but was received from the Lord.

Of this body of sacred teaching the apostles were the chosen interpreters and transmitters. The term 'apostolos', therefore, in its primary sense connotes more than a 'sent one'. The apostles were specially entrusted with a mission, and enriched by the Spirit of God with the needed equipment to fulfil their specific task. The apostles were a chosen number of Christ's disciples able to authenticate the events of Christ's life, and by the promised endowment of the Holy Spirit, to interpret and embody its significance for man's salvation. Their interpretation of the Christ-Event was part of the revealing fact. The apostolic men stood in close contact with Christ and for this reason they held a position historically unique. Yet it was not merely their proximity to Jesus which gave them their interpretation. They were men instructed by the Spirit; men who received the gift of interpreting knowledge from the ascended Lord. Their interpretation was his instruction. For this reason they, on their own account, gave commands in Christ's name. In their words, the act of historical divine revelation reached its goal; and so the circuit was made complete. It thus came about that for the first Christians

> the Holy Spirit and the apostles became correlative conceptions, with the consequence that the Scriptures of the New Testament were indifferently regarded as composed by the Holy Spirit or the apostles.[25]

In this regard the apostolic office, in its private and personal sense, was a temporary gift of the ascended Christ to his church (cf. Ephesians 4:11). The apostolate has in the New Testament itself a once-and-for-all character, as attesting the revelation in Christ and securing its content. The apostles had fulfilled their appointed task and historic mission when their testimony became inscripturated in the writings of the New Testament. It was through them that the gospel was embodied in a form which makes it available to every successive age, that men and women may come to saving faith in Christ through their word. For the plain fact is that,

> Any experience of God in Christ would have been impossible unless the meaning of 'Christ' were already fixed. And, ultimately, it can be fixed only by reference to the New Testament.[26]

For the first church, the writings of the apostolic interpreters and transmitters of the good news of God in Christ spoke with divine authenticity and authority. They vindicated and validated themselves in the experience of the single believer and in the life of the church as God's sure word. 'The New Testament is not Christ's book because it tells his story. It is his book because it is from him, born out of the wound of his heart, born like a child.'[27] In the apostolic writings the revelation in Christ reached its finality. And the revelatory significance of Christ's work is communicated through that written word to every generation. Thus to remain Christian is to reproduce the Christianity of the apostolic gospel and the apostolic church. 'For it is only through the apostles that we have received Christianity, and that Christianity *only* is genuine which can show itself to be *apostolic.*'[28]

How the several writings were brought together into a whole to form the New Testament as we have it comes under the subject of the New Testament canon, and lies outside our present concern. But, as Donald Guthrie observes:

> By the time of Irenaeus and Tertullian, the Christian churches generally were not only staunchly maintaining the Old Testament as scripture, but were also placing most of the New Testament books on an equal footing with it. There is sufficient positive evidence to show that most of the New Testament books were in authoritative use ... basically the Early Church was highly selective in its approach to Christian literature. The growth of competing gospels, acts, and other pseudoapostolic literature was not allowed to modify this basic approach. The books accepted were those which preserved apostolic doctrine.[29]

Within a comparatively short time, then, most of the New Testament writings, by virtue of their apostolic origin and internal spiritual force, had been gathered together. And by that time other writings of the subapostolic period had shown themselves to be of less significance for the church's faith and witness. Of these other writings, those carrying canonical status and revealing canonical stature could say in the words of John: 'they went out from us because they were not of us, for if they had been of us they would have remained with us.'

By putting the New Testament writings alongside the Old Testament and allowing them the designation 'scripture' in the same sense of that word as applied to the Old Testament, the early church expressed its faith in, and understanding of, its apostolic writings.

> The New Testament writings came to be part of the Bible only because they were joined to the Old Testament. For the earliest Christians holy Scripture was a known and established quantity.[30]

What Jesus and his disciples believed about the Old Testament, the apostolic church took to be equally applicable to its own corpus. Christ by his attitude to and use of the Old Testament validated its divinity, verified its historicity, and vindicated its authority. So too with the New Testament. If Moses and all the scriptures of the Old Testament speak of him; so also do the New Testament writings. They too come under the category of that action of the Holy Spirit which makes scripture what it is. As all Scripture is inspired by God, and as the New Testament is Scripture, so must it be Spirit-inspired.

It is therefore instructive to observe how it is possible to move from statements about Christ himself to like statements made about the scriptural words of the New Testament. Both, for example, reveal an eternal existence. Hebrews 13:8 declares Jesus Christ to be the same yesterday, today and forever. But so is the Word of God – the good news of the gospel – that which abides forever (cf. 1 Peter 1:25). Both partake of a human-divine aspect. Christ is '*God* manifest in the *flesh*' (1 Timothy 3:16); and concerning God's word it is specified, 'Holy *men* . . . spake as they were moved by the *Holy Spirit*.' Both reveal the same life-giving properties. In him is life (cf. John 1:14; 11:25; 2 Timothy 1:10; etc.): he is our life (1 Corinthians 3:4): and the word of God is living and powerful (Hebrews 4:12). Both are to be received as the condition of salvation: 'All who received him, who believed in his name, he gave power (authority) to become children of God.' (John 1:12.) The command is to 'receive with meekness the implanted word, which is able to save your souls' (James 1:21). Both are associated in the final judgement. In Acts 17:31 there is the apostolic declaration that Christ will judge the world in righteousness. Yet the dead will be judged according to those things written in the books (cf. Revelation 20:12; 22:19).

This parallel could, of course, be extended and amplified. But enough has been said to show that, as in the case of the Old Testament in which revelation and record dovetail, so it is with the New Testament. We may, at the risk of over-simplification, say that we have in the Old Testament the word and work of the Father for the sake of the Son, and in the New Testament the word and work of the Son for the sake of the Father. At any rate, the New Testament stands to the Old Testament in the relation of promise and fulfilment. The Old Testament records what 'God spake in time past unto the fathers by the prophets', whereas the New Testament records the final word spoken by the Son, in which the earlier revelation is summed up, confirmed, and transcended. So the New Testament presents a grand unity of teaching which is the perfect complement of the former inspired books which constitute the Old Testament; and which together form the Bible of the Christian church. The two Testaments are thus in the words of Thomas Watson 'the two lips of God by which God has spoken to us'.[31]

The close association stressed above between the early church and the scriptures raises the question of the relation between them. Undoubtedly the church was historically prior to the written word of the New Testament. But this fact does not admit the conclusion that the church is, therefore, pre-eminent to the scriptures. To be anterior does not prove an event to be superior. To be first is not to be final. The truth is that the church itself is the product of the preached apostolic word. It was the oral message which created the saved communities in which the apostolic word was regarded as authoritative. As long as this apostolic teaching was present and orally available, nothing more was required. As time passed, however, it became necessary to embody the apostolic message in permanent form. Thenceforward for the church the written word became equivalent to the spoken word, and thus the normative expression of the church's faith and its absolute authority in all things that pertain to life and godliness. In this way the New Testament is to be regarded as the true successor of the apostles. The apostles were the seat of authority at the first, and they have continued so to this day, the only difference being between their spoken and the written Word. The Word created the Church, not the Church the Word.[32]

The church is therefore bound to the scriptures for its final and absolute knowledge and authority in all that concerns its doctrines and its doings. Christ's work in its revelatory significance is transmitted and communicated by the written word. To suppose that saving knowledge comes to men apart from the scriptural word, that it is found in the church, would mean that there is no longer any necessity for the Bible. It is not the church itself which is infallible; but the scriptural word of God through which it was created and by which it lives. If, in fact, 'the church is infallible, it is impossible to understand why the Bible was given.'[33] The church has the Bible; and the Bible is the church's book.

The Books of the Bible were given *to* the Church more than *by* it, and they descended on it rather than rose from it. The Canon of the Bible rose from the Church, but not its content.[34]

Still the book is in the custody of the church; it is not in its control. For the church is only truly the church in its submission to the scripture as the word of God.

7
THE AUTHORITATIVE VOLUME

The question of authority is the most fundamental of all issues that concern the Christian church. It is indeed primary to all else. For if there is no objective authority, no sure word, no ultimate fact on which religious trust can repose and moral certainty rest, then it is left for each to believe and do what seems right in his own eyes. What is required is a final court of appeal, an absolute norm, to which Christian belief and behaviour can be referred. And from its beginning the church has looked to the Bible as meeting these requirements. For the church of Christ the scriptures of God have always been viewed as divinely authoritative.

The acknowledgement of the authority of the Bible is then basic to the acceptance of all that it has to teach, whether about justification by faith, the deity of Christ, or any other saving doctrine or ethical duty. Similarly, the recognition of the authority of scripture is primary to that of its inspiration. For if the Bible is accepted as speaking with the authority of God, and consequently true and trustworthy, then its statements about its own inspiration will receive the fullest credence. In this regard its authority becomes the key to its inspiration. Too often throughout history has the absolute truthfulness of scripture on points of interpretation and fact been called in question, then a doctrine of inspiration has been devised to make room for these alleged inconsistencies and inaccuracies. The following situation has thus arisen, as John MacLeod says:

> The campaign of opposition to the doctrine of the fully inspired character of Holy Writ, when it is carried on within the churches,

proceeds logically from a refusal to accept the *truth* of the claims which the Apostles made on their own behalf.[1]

In controversy with unbelievers it is not first the inspired character of scripture but its trustworthiness that is the issue. It is only when its truthfulness is acknowledged that there can be acceptance of its witness to what it says about its own origin. Faith in the Bible's authority is therefore a necessary presupposition for the acceptance of what the Bible has to say on any subject, and that authority derives directly from the biblical record itself.

The ground of authority

At the same time, and in justification for the order of the chapters in this volume, we must assert that, since the Bible presents and authenticates itself as involving God in its production, and is thus inspired verbally and fully, its authority can be said to derive directly from its claim to its one divine origin. It is not then inappropriate to appeal to the scriptures to validate their own authority. For as D. Martyn Lloyd-Jones truly affirms: 'The most important argument of all is that we should believe in the authority of the Scriptures because the Scriptures *themselves* claim that authority.'[2] There is no way then by which the question of the authority of the Bible can be dodged, for the Bible claims to instruct us for salvation (cf. 2 Timothy 3:15). It is therefore a matter of crucial importance for man's eternal destiny that it comes with a sure and certain word. The church of God lives under the authority of the word. And its every member is under the constant constraint to 'hear what the Spirit says to the churches' (cf. Revelation 3:22), to listen, that is, to the scriptures of God through which the Spirit still speaks to his church. For the Spirit's message comes through the medium of the written words (cf. Revelation 1:11; 2:1, etc.).

Although the idea of divine authority pervades the scriptures of the Old Testament, the word itself occurs only twice in the English versions (Proverbs 29:2, Hebrew *rabah*, and Esther 9:29, Hebrew *toqep*). But there are some instances where the Hebrew word *koaḥ*, usually translated 'power', could be rendered 'authority'. In the New Testament, the Greek word *exousia* is sometimes translated 'power' (AV), or 'right' (NEB), and sometimes 'authority'. The cogency of either rendering appears from an examination of such passages as Matthew 7:29; 9:6, 7; 28:18; John 1:12; 1 Corinthians 9:5; 2 Thessalonians 3:9. What emerges from a consideration of the various occurrences of the word is that the term *exousia* signifies power held by a right. In some contexts the emphasis falls on the *authority* which the possession of the power rightfully gives: in other instances it falls on the reality of the *power* which conditions the right use of authority.

To approach the subject of the authority of the Bible we must, however, begin with the final fact – with God himself. For all ultimate authority is located in him. And God alone is his own authority. Yet such ultimate authority cannot be proved, for there is nothing beyond the ultimate. God has in himself the only underived authority there can be. For there is nothing outside him on which his authority is founded. He is his own standard and norm. 'For when God made a promise to Abraham, since he had no one greater by whom to swear, he swore by himself.' (Hebrews 6:13.) 'God is the last authority for the religious,' says P. T. Forsyth, 'and therefore for the race, and he is the only authority we have in the end.'[3]

Yet while this ultimate authority of God cannot be proved, it can be recognized. For there is an *a priori* in man, not itself an authority but rather a capacity for authority. Man is essentially a responsible being before God. In the presence of God he discovers that his rightful attitude is that of a suppliant not a sovereign. Here he becomes aware that he does not exercise authority, he merely recognizes it. God is holy imperative. Man on the other hand has a receptivity for authority. Herein is his distinctiveness, his essential greatness. It is this fact about man which makes him of worth to God; and so worth saving even if never worthy of it. Before God the human will is aware of its true Master, and the human heart its only Lord. Where there is genuine faith in God as the source of man's being there will also be the recognition of God's absolute right over the whole area of

life. To believe in God is no less than to be committed to One
who claims the allegiance of one's whole nature. One is to be
'delivered, not from, but to, authority, though to a new kind of
authority'.[4] God stands for ever over against man as the one
absolute object of authority and not as the mere subject of man's
leisurely contemplation.

Final authority is, then, focused not upon the question, '*What*
is our authority?' but rather, '*Who* is our authority?'. For all
authority must be finally personal whatever be the impersonal
manner in which a specific requirement may reach us. Even such
a directive as 'Keep off the grass' has its ultimate reason in some
personal agent. Indeed, it seems that the acceptance of constraints is in ratio to the personal authority with which it is
backed. The marriage vow, for example, seems remote and
impersonal until we become involved. It is in the give and take of
personal relationships that such words as duty, obligation, and
ought, have meaning. The more intimately and personally
mediated they are, the more urgent and binding do they become.
The demands of religious faith and of ethical duty are therefore
incumbent upon us because they have their source and ground in
a personal God.

To ask the question, 'Who is our final authority?' admits
therefore of only one possible answer – God. Thus, to think
about absolute authority is to think about the personal rule of the
living God. But the God we know in Christian faith is not a Being
of sheer power. God's authority is the authority of what he is. It
is, therefore, basically a spiritual authority. It is 'what he
exercised by displaying, not his power, but his character.
Holiness, not omnipotence, is the spring of his spiritual
authority.'[5] In God unite kingship and fatherhood in his
character as holy-love. Thus does God present himself to us, as
H. H. Farmer says, 'in terms of succour and demand'.[6] As
created by him and for him God requires of man worship, love
and obedience. As man 'owns up' to the reality of God's
authority as the final court of appeal for his moral life, and 'owns'
that authority as the sure directive of his spiritual life, he makes
good his destiny as a moral and spiritual being. It is in this
recognition and acknowledgement that man, made in the image

of God, finds his true freedom in the God of the universe and the Lord of the cross.

> The problem of biblical authority, then, is a part of the problem of the authority of *God* over human life. If there is no God, and freedom means full and total human independence, then there is *no* authority; hence, there is no biblical authority.[7]

But God as personal Being, as we have shown, is disclosed in his revelation. God's authority is to be found there. Revelation is, therefore, the key to ultimate authority. God's authority and God's self-disclosure are thus two sides of the same reality. There can be no authority of God unless there is revelation; for in the locus of revelation is the seat of authority. In revelation the Object of faith is disclosed as authoritative. In a past age Augustine wrestled with the problem of authority, and urged on by the momentum of his own profound religious experience, he came to realize that revelation and authority are correlatives. In his self-disclosure God as Ultimate Authority speaks to man who has a receptivity for authority. In revelation it is the very God himself who comes authoritatively to man – actually, dramatic-ally, and savingly-disclosing his own being and character as the Triune God of all grace and power.

For the prophets of the Old Testament it was the revelation which gave them their authority. Their authority was not in their own person, but in the word they uttered. No subjective experience, no inner light, no illuminated imagination, gave them their authority. The word was their authority; the word which in coming to them reconciled them and recreated them, and made them ambassadors of God's authoritative revelation. For the Old Testament believers, the word of God's spokesmen came with authority. Thus it was that to disbelieve them was to disbelieve God, and to disobey them was to disobey him. They were not left to receive as authoritative just what appealed to them, but were called upon to accept all that was declared to them. For no moral being is his own authority. 'An authority which has its source in ourselves is no authority. In us authority can but have its echo, never its charter.'[8]

The authority of Jesus

For Christian faith Christ is the full and final revelation of God. Therefore in him has the authority of God found personal and permanent embodiment. In Christ, God's imperial authority is most graciously expressed. So is it that Warfield can contend that 'God's authoritative revelation is His gracious revelation; God's redemptive revelation is His supernatural revelation.'[9] Jesus Christ is then the summary of all that is authoritative for the life of man. It is central in the Christian gospel and vital for Christian experience to give unhesitating stress to Christ's finality. For in this finality of Christ is the authority of God. Thus 'the really big claim which is made in the whole of the New Testament is for the supreme authority of the Lord Jesus Christ'.[10] In its pages this authority of Christ is displayed and affirmed.

The first recorded comment on the teaching of Jesus in the New Testament is that the people 'were astonished at his teaching, for he taught them as one who had authority, and not as their scribes' (Matthew 7:28, 29; cf. Mark 1:21, 22). The Jews marvelled at the things he uttered, saying, 'How is it that this man has learning, when he has never studied?' (John 7:15). Unlike the rabbis of his time, he did not refer his statements to some accredited teacher of past days. If, indeed, Jesus quoted at all, it was from the Scriptures. But he constantly spoke on his own authority; or, more strictly, with the very authority of God; for he affirms that 'my teaching is not mine, but his who sent me' (John 7:16). His acts of healing displayed a divine authority. After assuring in his own name to a paralytic man the forgiveness of his sins, the crowds 'were afraid, and glorified God, who had given such authority to man' (Matthew 9:8). He performed his miraculous deeds with a commanding word (cf. Matthew 8:26, 27; Mark 9:25). He passed unmolested through a hostile crowd (Luke 4:28–30), and overthrew the tables of the money-lenders who disgraced the temple precincts (Matthew 21:12, 13) and so attested his moral authority; while his riding into Jerusalem on an ass was a demonstration of regal authority (cf. Matthew 22:1–11; Zechariah 9:9). His acts of mercy on the sabbath day, which led him to declare against the legalism of Pharisaism, that 'the sabbath was made for man, and not man for the sabbath' (Mark 2:27), showed his sovereignty in the realm of religion.

The absoluteness of Christ's authority in the sphere of ultimate knowledge of God is asserted in Matthew 11:27; as is a like ultimate authority in the realm of a complete knowledge of man implied in John 2:25. Commenting on Jesus' parable of the two builders (cf. Matthew 7:24–27; Luke 6:47–49), William Barclay concludes, 'It is Jesus' claim that he is the only sure foundation for life. Life founded on any other foundation will be swept away by the storms of life.'[11] Christ possessed the power to forgive human sin (Matthew 9:1–8); and the authority to judge the world (Matthew 25:31–46; John 5:22). His words of call to his disciples (Matthew 10:1; cf. Mark 3:13; Luke 6:13), and about the cost of being his disciples (cf. Matthew 10:34–39; Luke 14:26, 27; 9:59, 60; Matthew 10:38, 39; 16:24, 25; Mark 8:34, 35; Luke 9:23, 24; 17:33), reveal in Christ a consciousness of authority far beyond and above the ordinary. For 'no man ever spoke like this man!' (John 7:46).

In what did this consciousness of his unique authority lie? Not simply in the novelty of his teaching, or in his manner of presenting truths. Nor was it the right, legal or ecclesiastical, to speak which gave his words their authority. It was not because he was exceptionally clever as against the doctors of the law. For they were not stupid men. They had earned their title by long study and wide knowledge. The authority of Jesus had another source and ring about it, 'unlike the doctors of the law' (cf. Mark 1:22, NEB). Christ's authority was something other than that gained in the schools. In two great sayings in John's gospel there is surely disclosed the source of this unique authority of Christ. 'Do you not believe that I am in the Father and the Father in me? The words that I say to you I do not speak on my own authority; but the Father who dwells in me does his works,' (John 14:10), and, 'I and the Father are one' (John 10:30).

His oneness with the Father in the reality of his being is the source of his teaching. His words are thus nothing other than the words of deity; nothing less on his lips than the affirmation of a divine authority. The authority of Jesus Christ is the authority of God – no other and no less than that. What he was in himself gave his words their authority. His filial union with the Father was the basis from, and context in which he spoke. In him the authority of God was innate. As the Word made flesh he was, and remains, God's truth for life's way – for the whole world.

Christ came among men as embodying the ultimate authority of God. In this regard the great 'I am' passages in the fourth gospel have a special significance. In some Old Testament passages the term is used as a colourless statement of identity (cf. Genesis 45:3). But in other passages it is said to have 'the style of deity' (cf. e.g. Genesis 17:1; Exodus 3:14; 15:26; Psalm 35:3; Isaiah 43:11, 13, 25; 51:12; 61:8). In these references the 'I am' is a characteristic of God. So Christ affirms himself the 'I am' as the 'bread of life' (John 6:35); 'the light of the world' (John 8:12); 'the door of the sheep' (John 10:7, 9); 'the good shepherd' (John 10:11); 'the resurrection and the life' (John 11:25); 'the way, the truth, and the life' (John 14:6); and 'the true vine' (John 15:1).

All these 'I am' sayings speak in the style of divinity, and in the accent of God. Peter's speech betrayed him to be of Galilee; Christ's speech revealed him to be of God. He was among men as the incarnate authority of God for the direction of men's lives and the settling of their destiny. Therefore we say that God's revelation is the disclosure of his authority. And that revelation, reaching its full expression and final embodiment in Jesus Christ our Lord, places him as absolute authority in all the concerns of human life under God. Christ is for all men a regal authority who has brought into human history a regal redemption. For he is at once the epitome of the presence of God as grace and truth. It is therefore precisely 'because truth as found in Christ is unique, the Christian faith claims for itself an absolute and universal character'.[12] And this sovereignty of Christ means that

> we are under his orders, and his orders are based on the fact that he has absolute right over us in conducting our lives.[13]

His name is exalted above all other names; and as Lord over the total world he possesses all authority in heaven and on earth by an absolute right (Philippians 2:9–11; Matthew 28:18).

One of the good points of much recent and contemporary theology is this emphasis on the unique authority of Christ. But it has sometimes been stated so as to disallow authority to the scriptures. Thus, for example, a New Testament scholar of the calibre of William Barclay emphatically rejects the authority of the Bible on the score that 'for the Christian there is only one authority, and that authority is Jesus Christ interpreted by the Holy Spirit'.[14] But instead of the authority of Christ making void the authority of scripture, it rather establishes it. To say vaguely that Christ is our authority leaves the issue in confusion.[15] For the immediate question is, what Christ? The Christ who is final and authoritative is neither the Christ of varying experience nor of a mutilated Bible. When, therefore, we say Christ is our authority we need to understand that there is only one Christ, namely, the biblical Christ. We cannot know Christ at all if we do not know the scriptures; and we do not know the scriptures if we fail to find Christ. To know Christ is to know God in the biblical revelation. It is, that is to say, to own the authority of God in his revelation in Christ through the scriptures. It is consequently impossible to speak of an authoritative Christ apart from the scriptures in which he is set forth; in the Old Testament prefigured, and in the New presented. The Old Testament preparation for the revelation of God in Christ is no mere ornamental prefix to it, nor is the apostolic interpretation of God's revealed will in Christ a mere addition to it. They are essential to it, and as such share in God's revelatory authority.

Both the historical preparation for the Christ event, and the apostolic interpretation of the Christ fact, are essential for a full estimate of the Christ who alone is absolute. We do not know Christ by the delineation of the historical Jesus alone, nor yet do we know him by focusing on the Christ of faith alone. There is no understanding of the historical Jesus apart from faith's affirmations; and, on the other hand, faith's affirmations are of a Jesus genuinely historical. It is, therefore, as P. T. Forsyth was fond of stressing, the whole biblical Christ that is the truly and deeply historical Christ.

The apostolic interpretation of God's authoritative revelation in Christ is not an addition to the revelation; it is an integral part of it. In the apostolic interpretation God's revelation in Christ is finalized. It must therefore be evident that to acknowledge that Christ is final and authoritative is at the same time to acknowledge that the scriptures are final and authoritative.

It is frequently pointed out by those who would detract from the authority of the Bible that Jesus never wrote a book. But the observation is not pertinent to the present discussion, for it would be a dangerous conclusion to draw that he never wanted his teaching and the understanding of his mission written down. And anyway he did, as the risen Lord, command his servant John to write concerning him 'in a book' (Revelation 1:11; cf. 22:7f). The fact is, of course, that God's revelation could not have been embodied in a book until that revelation was fully known and made fully comprehensible. Our Lord could hardly explain and expound the significance of his coming until the crowning event itself was accomplished. It was the business of his chosen apostles, as his posthumous penmen, under the inspiration of the Holy Spirit, to state and safeguard the revelation. The apostles were men with a unique vocation; they were God's 'elect and providential personalities' who spoke in the name of the ascended Lord as his unconditional legitimate vehicles. These apostolic men were not corrupters of God's self-disclosure in Christ; they were its conveyers. Their words were not an intrusion upon the revelation, but a part of its schema.

Therefore Christ has fulfilled himself in the words of the apostles, so that their words are his. What he was unable to say to them in the days of his flesh, he now in reigning glory, by the mouth of the Spirit, communicates to them. There is no Christ for Christian faith but the Christ whom we know in the Bible. And being shut up to the pages of the written word, we are *ipso facto* bound by its authority. For the authority of God's revelation disclosed finally in Christ is perpetuated in the written word. The Bible, then, indispensably participates in the authority of the living Christ.

Authority in the written word

Thus do the scriptures embody God's revealed authority for the faith, life and guidance of both the individual and the church. God comes new to every age in his revelation in Christ, in the words of scripture. Here in the Bible he actually speaks his will which is authoritative for every generation.

When the Bible itself is examined it discloses throughout evidences and statements of its divine authority. Jesus, as we have seen, regarded the Old Testament as the word of God, and submitted to its authority. In his encounter with Satan in the wilderness of temptation he settled every question by reference to what was written. And he carried through his mission in the consciousness that he fulfilled its prophetic word. This fact of fulfilled prophecy is a compelling mark of its authority. For Jesus the scriptures were final in all matters of controversy. The Sadducees erred in their denial of a resurrection of the dead because they neither knew the scriptures, nor the power of God (Matthew 22:29).

The New Testament too is stamped with divine authority through the apostolicity of its authors. They were men who had a special call to be eyewitnesses to the reality of Christ (cf. John 15:27; Acts 1:2; 1 Corinthians 9:1; 15:8, 9; 2 Corinthians 12:12; Galatians 1:14; Hebrews 2:3, 4; 1 Peter 5:1; 1 John 1:1–5) and appointed to a unique ministry by the ascended Lord as the custodians of the gospel (cf. Ephesians 4:10f.). What Paul says in reference to the communion service, 'For I received from the Lord what I also delivered to you,' (1 Corinthians 11:23) may be taken as applicable to all his declarations, and to be equally true of the statements of the other New Testament writers. Paul tells the Thessalonians that 'when you received the word of God which you heard from us, you accepted it not as the word of men but as what it really is, the word of God' (1 Thessalonians 2:13). And he affirms that he is 'accursed' who dare preach any gospel other than what he preaches (Galatians 1:8). For 'my gospel', as he speaks of it (Romans 2:16; 16:25) is none other than the 'gospel of God' (Mark 1:14; Romans 1:1; 15:16; 2 Corinthians 11:7; 1 Thessalonians 2:2; 2:9; 1 Peter 4:17; cf. 2 Timothy 1:11);

of Christ (Mark 1:1; Romans 15:16; 1 Corinthians 9:12; 2 Corinthians 2:12; 9:13; 10:14; Galatians 1:7, etc.); the veritable gospel of the grace of God (Acts 20:24). Whoever is of God, John declares, will listen to the word of God's apostolic men (1 John 4:6). For such men have the right 'to command and exhort in the Lord Jesus Christ' (2 Thessalonians 3:4, 6, 10, 12, 14). Therefore is the church built and established upon 'the foundation of the apostles and prophets' (Ephesians 2:20f).

It is this apostolic authority which underlies and undergirds the whole New Testament and establishes its authority in God. For in the words of scripture, whether spoken by God himself, or declared by an inspired prophet or apostle, the actual authority of God in Christ through the Holy Spirit is made perpetually vocal. To believe, then, the biblical word is to believe in Christ and so to be brought into the common faith of the people of God in every generation, and made one with them in the historic gospel. 'He believed fundamentally in the gracious word of God revealed to man, as over-riding and over-ruling all authorities,' says A. Taylor Innes of John Knox.[16] In this same biblical faith all Christians have their oneness in Christ.

We are bidden of late to beware of a ' "Bible-only" mentality' on the score that scripture is not the totality of all God has said and done in the world.[17] But is not the Bible itself the authority for this fact? It does declare the reality of God's actions in the whole world. It is, of course, correct to declare that

> Christ was crucified for our sins whether that was ever recorded in a book or not; Christ arose from the dead whether that ever be made a topic of written testimony.[18]

But would we ever be sure of our knowing that he was crucified and risen if that were not recorded in a book? We could hardly have come to believe that it was 'for our sins' he died, if that interpretation were not given to apostolic men by the Holy Spirit and made a topic of written testimony. It is only in the scriptural record we have the authority for these realities of the gospel. Without it we are shut up to tradition or experience. And both of these have proved themselves to be uncertain authorities. The easy way of dismissing this assertion of biblical authority is to brand it 'fundamentalism', and then to charge with Jürgen Moltmann that 'fundamentalism fossilizes the Bible into an unquestioned authority'.[19] But for Moltmann, who sets himself the task of expounding the significance of the cross as the central issue in the Christian message, it is an ill-considered remark. For it undercuts all that he has to say in his otherwise challenging book. He seeks to establish his thesis on the basis of the scripture; and, indeed, on the verbal form of certain passages. But what if its statements are not to be given credence? What if it only provides a questionable authority? If some elements of the biblical word are to be declared unsure, then its authority is in question. But the burden of proof is on those who so regard it to chronicle these deficiencies so that they may be eliminated from the record. Any author in whose book inexact statements are proved to exist would for the sake of his own credibility and that of his work want them brought to light so that they may be corrected in a later edition. Why then, do not those who are sure that the Bible contains inexactitudes edit a new edition from which these errors are eliminated; or, perhaps, provide a sheet of *errata* for existing volumes? Thielicke sees the 'Fall' of man as his renunciation of the supremacy of God. He presents Eve as desiring to remain a devout lady engaging in a religious discussion with the serpent. 'Eve and the serpent are simply exchanging views on the question whether God actually said this or that, whether what he said is properly documented.'[20] Maybe the question posed is the same for every age: Has God spoken? It is the essence of Christian faith to believe that he has, and that his word comes to us in the scriptures with his authority.

Yet there is a danger to be avoided in this stress on the Bible's authority as inspired and infallible. It is all too easy for it to become formulized into a 'wooden orthodoxy'. The post-reformation Lutheran and Calvinist dogmaticians were so intent on defining the principle of *sola scriptura* (scripture alone) that they became the cause of this doctrine losing

> much of the validity and profundity of the reformers' interpretation of the Scriptures, however. Divine inspiration became for them more a matter of intellectual assent than, as for Luther, an ever-

fresh experience of hearing the Holy Spirit speak through the Bible's pages.[21]

Before proceeding further, says Calvin at the opening of chapter seven of the first book of his *Institutes*, 'it seems proper to make some observations on the authority of Scripture.' He proceeds thereupon to show that the authority of scripture is not given by anything outside itself. Its authority lies within itself as God's word. 'Scripture bears upon the face of it as clear evidence of its truth as white and black do of their colours, sweet and bitter of their taste.' As scripture, the Bible partakes in and communicates the life of God. For no book can do the miracles this book does unless God be with it. When we think of the matter the Bible contains it is hard to escape the conclusion that here is something quite beyond what the human mind could have conceived. As Thomas Boston says,

> The mystery of Scripture is so profound that no man or angel could have known it, had it not been divinely revealed. That eternity should be born, that he who thunders in the heavens should cry in a cradle; that he who rules the stars should suck the breasts; that the Prince of Life should die; that the Lord of Glory should be put to shame; that sin should be punished to the full, yet pardoned to the full; who could ever have conceived of such a mystery had not the Scriptures revealed it to us? [22]

God may have more light to break forth from his word; but he has no more light to give apart from his word. We can never grow beyond these everlasting words; we can only grow into them more deeply.

We have seen that the authority of God revealed in Christ has been embodied in the written word. But this authority is mediated by the Holy Spirit. The next chapter will have something to say on the relation between the Spirit and the word. For the present we need only emphasize the action of the Spirit in mediating the authority of the word. The Spirit brought the biblical writings into being, and what is written is thus the voice of the Spirit. To hear the voice of the Spirit in the scriptures is, therefore, at one with acknowledging the authority of the written word. In this actuality of the Spirit God's authority is made factual in the scriptures. The authority of the Bible rests upon the fact that here in its words the revelation of God in Christ comes to life through the Spirit for each successive age.

But this authority of God's revelation in the written word must be appropriated in Christian experience and acknowledged in the church. By the individual God's authority is appropriated by faith. Indeed, faith may be defined as the illumination of God's revelation by the Spirit which brings man into a responsive acceptance of God's authority in the word. For the believer, then, the scripture becomes his authority; and he will consequently seek to live in the obedience of faith according to its requirements. This does not make experience itself the ground of authority. To make the individual his own authority is to be guilty of confusing the appropriation with the actuality. Every believing man must see his authority in the revelation of God as this is centralized in the life and work of Jesus Christ and finalized and perpetuated in the holy scriptures.

> If the living God has spoken, His word of revelation is the authority in religion. If this word is made permanent in writing, then the written revelation is our authority in religion. A man accepts this written revelation as his authority in religion by personal appropriation. But whatever the subjective ground for receiving this revelation might be, it neither constitutes nor comprises the authority of the divine revelation.[23]

And the church, too, will be true to its high calling in God only as it submits to the authority of the word. For the church is the community of those who have appropriated the authority of Christ and acknowledged his sovereign reality. As the body of Christ (1 Corinthians 1:18; cf. 2:19; Ephesians 1:23, 4:12, etc.) and the building of God (1 Corinthians 3:9, cf. 14:12; Ephesians 2:21, 22), the church has its creation in the biblical revelation, and exists for its communication. Its *raison d'être* is in and for the gospel. The church has no authority in and of itself; it has its authority through and under the word of God.

> The Bible is not dependent for its authority upon the church, although the Bible comes to us with the commendation of the church as its standard and rule of faith. The Bible is not dependent

for its authority upon the church because the gospel to which it witnesses is not the creation of the church or subservient to its decisions. On the contrary, the gospel has brought the church into being and keeps the church in obedience to God. If the witness of the Bible to the gospel of the grace of God in Jesus Christ is untrustworthy, then nothing whatever can build up the church again. If the thought, structure, and institutions of the church's life are not really subject to the witness of the Bible, but are determined by the influence of some other reality, then the church has betrayed its trust. The church must again and again search the Scriptures of the Old and New Testaments, for these are they which testify of Jesus Christ as Lord.[24]

The statement of the church's doctrine must be in harmony with, and the shape of the church's life must be congruous to the biblical testimony. For the nerve-centre of this testimony is precisely this: the lordship of God, in the revelation of Christ, assured by the written word, over the church, and in the personal existence of every believer. Whatever has not its warrant and mandate either directly or by rightful deduction from these oracles of God is not binding on any man whose true freedom is to be found under that authority. George Wishart, the early master of John Knox, appended to his translation of the First Helvetic or Swiss Confession, the following words which are not in either the Latin or German original:

> It is not in our mind for us to prescribe by these brief chapters a certain rule of the faith to all churches and congregations, for we know no other rule of faith but the Holy Scriptures.

This statement is altogether right both in what it refuses to accept as authoritative for the people of God, and in what it affirms as the true locus of that authority.

In its reality as the word of God the Bible has its absolute authority. And in that reality it has its adequacy, finality and infallibility. In this conviction the Bible is to be heard (Exodus 19:9; Numbers 9:8; Deuteronomy 4:1f.; 5:1f.; Joshua 3:9, etc.; Psalm 66:16; 85:8, etc.; Ezekiel 20:47, etc.; Acts 2:22; 13:7, etc.); read (cf. Deuteronomy 17:19; Jeremiah 36:6f.; Matthew 20:3f.; 21:42; Acts 8:28f; Ephesians 3:4; Colossians 4:16; 1 Thessalonians 5:27; 1 Timothy 4:13; Revelation 1:3); studied

(Ezekiel 7:10; Nehemiah 8:13; cf. Psalm 119:48, 78, 148; Ezekiel 3:12; 2 Timothy 2:15); believed (2 Chronicles 20:20; Psalm 106:12; 119:16; Luke 1:20; John 4:4f.; 5:46f.; etc., Acts 4:4f., etc., 2 Thessalonians 1:10, etc.); loved (Joshua 22:5; Psalm 40:16; 70:4; 119:47, 48, 97, 119, 127, 159, 163, 165; John 14:15f., etc.); and obeyed (Deuteronomy 4:30; 11:13f., etc.; 1 Kings 6:12, etc.; Jeremiah 7:23, etc.; Ezekiel 11:20, etc.; John 3:31; Acts 5:29f.; 2 Thessalonians 1:8; 3:14; Hebrews 5:9; 1 Peter 4:17; 1 John 5:2).

The word of God's authority is thus a 'lamp' for times of uncertainty, illuminating the next step of the way (Psalm 119:105; cf. 2 Samuel 22:29; Psalm 132:17; Proverbs 6:23; 2 Peter 1:19), and a 'light', throwing its brightening rays on the more distant path for those needing direction (Psalm 119:105, 130; cf. Psalm 27:1; 118:27; Isaiah 60:19; Luke 2:32; 2 Corinthians 4:4; Ephesians 5:8, 9). It is like a 'hammer', breaking open the hardened heart (Jeremiah 23:29), and like 'fire', consuming in its purifying flame life's useless dross (Jeremiah 23:29; cf. Isaiah 66:15f.; Hebrews 12:29); and it is like 'honey', sweetening the bitternesses of life's experiences (Psalm 119:103; Psalm 19:10; cf. Psalm 119:103; 81:16; see Ezekiel 3:3). In the hands of men of faith it is a swift-acting sword for victory in the battle with evil (Ephesians 6:17; cf. Hebrews 4:12; Revelation 1:16; 2:12, 16; 19:15, 21). And for all it is an ever-fresh spring assuaging human thirst (of. Amos 8:11; Isaiah 55:1; Jeremiah 2:13; John 4:13f; 7:27) and cleansing away the dark stains of sin (John 15:13; cf. Ephesians 5:16; Titus 3:5). It is as nursing milk for spiritual babes (Hebrews 5:12, cf. 1 Corinthians 3:2) and nourishing meat for the mature (Hebrews 5:14; cf. John 4:32, 34).

These realities of God's word bring the Bible into dynamic relation to life. For the authority of God is not that of God in the abstract, but of God in his revelation. Life is truly lived only under the lordship of God in Christ through the word. This constant interaction of the theological truth regarding the Bible and the experimental apprehension of it is necessary for a full understanding of its authority as holy scripture. 'Man shall not live by bread alone, but by every word that proceeds from the mouth of God.' (Matthew 4:4.)

For whatever was written in former days was written for our instruction, that by steadfastness and by the encouragement of the scriptures we might have hope. (Romans 15:4.)

8
THE SPIRIT AND THE WORD

The Christian doctrine of the Holy Spirit, it has been said, arose out of the experience of the church as it interpreted, and is itself interpreted by, the promise of the *Paraclete* given by Jesus in John 14–16. While the presence of the Spirit was foreshadowed in God's particular relation to Israel, his special indwelling was for Christians a new experience (cf. John 7:39; Acts 2:1f.). And the Spirit's relationship to the incarnate Word was for the early church 'a new factor in the world's history', and was understood in proportion as Christ was seen to realize in himself the messianic promise and hope. Christ himself asserted this identity by declaring that upon him the Spirit of the Lord had come in fulfilment of Isaiah's prophecy (Luke 4:18; cf. Isaiah 61:1, 2; see Luke 3:21, 22; 4:1). And his own ministry may be summed up in the declaration of Mark 1:8, 'He shall baptize you in the Holy Spirit.' Thus can the NEB translate the text of Romans 8:9 like this: 'If a man does not possess the Spirit of Christ, he is no Christian.'

The Spirit in the Old Testament

Yet while the presence of the Spirit in these new relationships is distinctive of the gospel dispensation, the fact of the Spirit's reality was common to the faith of the people of God throughout the Old Testament period. His universal presence was declared in such statements as Psalm 139:7, 'Whither shall I go from thy Spirit? Or where shall I flee from thy presence?' In this soliloquy of the psalmist, God's Spirit is identified with God's presence (cf. Psalm 51:11). Foreshadowed, too, in God's particular relation to the nation of Israel, and his specific action in and through those who communicated to her his revelatory acts and words, is his special association with the church of Christ in the New Testament. When, therefore, Paul addressed himself to the disciples in Ephesus he did not speak to them of believing in the Holy Spirit, but of receiving the Holy Spirit when they believed (Acts 19:2).

The Old Testament does not, in fact, use the single term 'the Holy Spirit'. In two places the epithet 'holy' is found as a prefix to that of 'Spirit', but in each case it is further qualified by a possessive pronoun, 'thy holy Spirit' (Psalm 51:11), and 'his holy Spirit' (Isaiah 63:10). It is still true to say, however, that mention of the Spirit of God, or the Spirit of the Lord, is frequent in the Old Testament, and is found in every part of it. Common to it is the idea of the Spirit of Yahweh (Jehovah) going forth from him, to accomplish his works in the world and among men as his life-giving word. Significant, therefore, is the parallel between the Spirit and the word throughout the scriptures. All through there stands out this vital parallelism between the divine breath, wind, or spirit, on the one side, and the divine voice, mouth, or word, on the other. Schultz has observed that the conception of 'Spirit' is characteristic of the Old Testament being closely associated with the 'word'.[1] The distinction between the two is that between the 'breath' and 'voice' of God. The voice is the articulate expression of thought, whereas the breath is the force through which the word is made a living actuality. Thus the Spirit in the scriptures of the old economy is the life of God communicated by a word. 'By the word of the Lord were the heavens made, and the host of them by the breath of his mouth.' (Psalm 33:6; cf. Psalm 51:11; 104:30; 139:7.)

God's Spirit and God's word are seen in this parallelism in the work of creation. Genesis 1:2–3 puts the 'hovering' of the Spirit adjacent to the utterance of God – 'And God said'. In fact, as Thomas Rees observes, in the story of creation 'the agency of the Spirit is extended to the whole framework and order of creation'.[2] The passage quoted above from Psalm 33 (verse 6) brings the two operations, that of the Spirit and the word into the same parallel. While Psalm 104:30 affirms, 'When thou sendest forth thy Spirit they are created.' The RSV has a capital S for

Spirit, and gives the marginal alternative 'Breath'. The combination 'word' and 'wind' is found in Psalm 147:18. The Spirit and the word are, then, in Irenaeus' beautiful phrase the 'two hands of God' through which he framed the world.

No less in God's revelatory action in the Old Testament is this significant parallelism between the Spirit and the word to be discerned. The nation of Israel was chosen of God to fulfil a divine purpose. She was not chosen for any merit she possessed, but to be a vehicle of God's disclosure of his saving plan for a lost world. A special endowment of God's Spirit was given to the Hebrew nation which constituted her a prophetic people, and, as such, the chosen organ of the divine unveiling. Israel is thus the 'anointed' of God (cf. Psalm 105:15). But this anointing passed to the leaders of the people as specially called of God and endowed by his Spirit to bring Israel to fulfil her part in God's scheme. Thus were Israel and those who guided her destiny the objects of God's 'preferential action', through the Spirit, and so the channel of his revelation, the 'mouth' through which God made his will known (cf. Exodus 4:16).

More specifically, however, the Spirit of God spoke by the mouth of God's holy prophets. In the relationship between the divine Spirit and the prophetic word the distinctive parallelism of Spirit and word comes out most clearly. In the early period of Israel's history, the presence of the Spirit was regarded as the spirit of prophecy; in later Judaism the Spirit of God and the spirit of prophecy became almost identical. Consequently, from the first to the last communication of God to the prophets, God's revelation was conceived to be a direct and living communication by the Spirit of the Voice of God. Through Spirit and word, God himself was seen working and heard speaking. Thus at the end of his message to the house of Jacob in which Isaiah speaks *words* in God's name, the prophet declares, 'And now the Lord has sent me and his Spirit' (Isaiah 48:16). And Zechariah referring to the former prophets asserts that they proclaimed 'the words which the Lord of hosts had sent by his Spirit' (Zechariah 7:12).

God's word and Spirit, then, parallel in the reality of God's presence. God's presence goes with those who keep his word (cf. Exodus 33:14; Psalm 16:11; 33:4; 119:42, 81; 130:5), and with such his Spirit abides (cf. Job 33:4; Psalm 51:10, 11, 12; 143:10). So too do the word and Spirit parallel in the actuality of God's power. The word which goes forth from his mouth accomplishes his purpose and prospers in the thing for which he sent it (Isaiah 55:11; cf. Psalm 147:5). God made the earth by his power, and established the world by his wisdom, and by his understanding stretched out the heavens (Jeremiah 51:15). Not by human might or power is God's plan brought to final issue (cf. Deuteronomy 8:17), but by his Spirit (Zechariah 4:6). So the prophet Micah, in fulfilling the divine commission, declares himself to be full of power by the Spirit of the Lord (Micah 3:8).

The Spirit in the New Testament

In the New Testament this significant parallelism continues. To both word and Spirit are attributed the same functions and results. The background here may be Ezekiel's vision of the dry bones. The dry bones were symbolic of a people ruined and dead. The prophet was brought by the Spirit of the Lord and set down in the midst of the valley (Ezekiel 37:1) and there commanded to speak God's word (cf. verses 4, 5). Later the Lord declares, 'I will put my Spirit within you, and you shall live' (verse 14). Here the spoken word and the acting Spirit operate, and the result is a new creation.

In some such way we have throughout the New Testament the same suggestive parallelism between word and Spirit, in which, so to speak, the revivifying of the dry bones is attributed indifferently either to the 'Spirit' or to the 'word'. In John 3:8, for example, the new birth is related to the action of the Spirit; while in 1 Peter 1:23, it is declared that we are 'born anew . . . through the living and abiding word'. We are sanctified either 'by the Spirit' (1 Peter 1:2), or, 'in the truth; thy word is truth' (John 17:17). Peter in addressing the Council of Jerusalem points out that the Gentiles' hearts are cleansed through faith by the Holy Spirit given to them, as to the earlier Jewish believers (Acts 15:7ff.). In John 15:3 we are said to be made clean by the word spoken by the Lord. Especially significant, because in the same context, are the statements of John 6. At verse 63 there is the declaration that 'it is the Spirit which gives life'; while later (verse 68) Peter answers our Lord's enquiry, 'Will you also go away?' with the reply, 'Lord, to whom shall we go? You have the *words* of eternal life.' In fact, the earlier verse (63) continues with the affirmation of Christ that the words he has spoken are spirit and life. By the Spirit, according to 1 John 3:24, we have an understanding of things divine, while in Titus 1:9 such an understanding is attributed to the word. By the Spirit or by the word is the ultimate judgement. And it is by being indwelt by the Spirit or by the word that we truly abide in Christ.

But not only is there this significant parallelism between the Spirit and the word; there is also a vital connection between them. And this inter-relationship of the Spirit holds good whether the context is that of the Word incarnate, the word written, or the word proclaimed.

We have seen that Christ is the Word of God in an absolute sense. And yet between the Word made flesh and the Holy Spirit there is an inter-relationship. Throughout the New Testament the life and work of Jesus stand in the very closest relation to the Holy Spirit. The account and interpretation of this fact belong to the doctrine of the person of Christ, but it is necessary here to point out the fact. It seems clear that Jesus, the Word made flesh, experienced an indwelling of the Spirit for the perfecting of his life as man and an enduement of the Spirit for the fulfilment of his office as Messiah. Thus was the Spirit's effect both personal and ministerial. All that it was necessary for him to possess in virtue of his human nature was imparted to him unstintingly by the Spirit. As the Word of God incarnate, Jesus was no less a man. There was no masquerading of divine omnipotence in human frailty. Therefore, since God has made man by his Spirit, and man only truly lives in dependence upon God's Spirit, it follows that Jesus, if he was authentically one with mankind, must have depended upon God's indwelling and enabling.

Thus when Christ assumed the role of Messiah he identified himself with the Servant of the Lord upon whom the Spirit of the Lord came. Born of the Spirit, Jesus grew in spirit. The Spirit secured that his human flesh, derived from Mary, should not become the basis of sin's operation. All through the days of his earthly ministry, Jesus was under the constant and penetrating influence of the Spirit of God. Developed in manhood through the Spirit, he went forth anointed to fulfil his messianic task. He cast out Satan by the Spirit of God (Matthew 12:28), and declared the words of God through the same Spirit (John 3:34). The Spirit remained with him throughout the span of his earthly life, controlling his mind, will, and actions, so that he learned from God, acted for God, taught of God, unto the fulness of the stature of a perfect man. And at the end he offered himself as a sacrifice acceptable and well-pleasing to God, through the eternal Spirit (Hebrews 9:14). There is, therefore, nothing strange, nothing incongruous, in Peter's declaration in the home of Cornelius that Jesus was among men as one 'anointed with the Holy Spirit and with power' (Acts 10:38; cf. 4:27; Luke 4:18).

In experience, this vital tie between Spirit and word remains. Subjectively, to be a Christian is to receive Christ (John 1:12), and to receive the Spirit (Galatians 3:5): here is the significant parallelism. But we cannot receive Christ the Word but by the Spirit; for it is the Spirit who takes of the things of Christ and reveals them unto us. And no man can call Jesus, Lord, in the saving sense, except by the Spirit (1 Corinthians 12:3). Such is the vital relationship between the Spirit and the word. It is the Spirit who reproduces in the believer the life of Christ. So we can say with James Denney, that 'Christian life and life in the Spirit are one thing'. The Word gave up his life *for us* through the Spirit; and the Spirit gives the life of the Word *to us* – through the scriptures.

This observation leads us on to the relationship between the Spirit and the written word. Here two such connections are important: one, the Spirit in the process of the inspiration of the written word; the other, the Spirit in the crisis of the illumination of that same word.

The inspiration of the Spirit

Something has been already said on the first of these issues in chapter 4, and we shall avoid being repetitious here. 'The Bible,' declares Theodore Mueller, 'is very emphatic in witnessing that the divine truth of salvation has been mediated to men by the Holy Spirit both orally and in the Scriptures'[3]. So close and vital indeed is the Spirit's connection with the written word that it is indifferent whether we assert the Holy Spirit says, or the scripture says (cf. Hebrews 3:7). The Holy Spirit is represented in scripture itself as the mouthpiece of the Lord through whom the word of the Lord was given perpetual embodiment in written form. The apostle Paul states emphatically that what he sets forth in his epistle is what 'God has revealed through the Spirit'; and this he 'imparts in words not of human wisdom, but taught by the Spirit, interpreting spiritual truths to those who possess the Spirit' (1 Corinthians 2:10, 13). Throughout the Bible the creation of Scripture is uniformly attributed to the action of the Holy Spirit. David spoke his words 'in the Spirit' (Matthew 22:43). Peter affirms categorically that it was the Holy Spirit who spoke beforehand by the mouth of David (Acts 1:16). Paul asserts that the Holy Spirit was right in speaking to the fathers of his people through the prophets (Acts 28:25). Prophecy of old came not by human impulse, but by the movement of God's Spirit (2 Peter 1:11); and those who uttered it 'inquired what person or time was indicated by the Spirit of Christ within them when predicting the sufferings of Christ and the subsequent glory' (1 Peter 1:11). So is the Spirit the divine mediator of the written word; the word which fully and infallibly assures the saving benefits of the Word incarnate.

> This means that the Holy Spirit does not testify by the written Word anything against Christ, the incarnate Word. The two are never in opposition to each other, but always bear witness to each other. The written Word is the divinely inspired revelation concerning the incarnate Word, the Saviour of sinners, by which the Holy Spirit is operative towards their salvation.[4]

What then is Scripture but 'literature indwelt by the Spirit of God'?[5] We are constantly urged to treat the Bible as literature, a sort of spiritual classic, a collection of holy thoughts of God-intoxicated men. But this is not how the Bible presents itself. Of course, the Bible is literature, the work of men. But it is also *divine* literature. Literature is the letter; scripture is the letter inspired by the Spirit. What Jesus said of the new birth holds in reference to the scriptures: 'That which is born of the flesh is flesh, but that which is born of the Spirit is Spirit.' For 'it is the Spirit that gives life, the flesh is of no avail; the words that I have spoken to you are spirit and life' (John 6:63). 'Words they were, and in that respect, literature; but words divinely inbreathed and therefore Scripture.'[6] We may say, therefore, with Luther, that 'the Bible is the very language of the Spirit',[7] or with Augustine, who declares that at his conversion 'with great avidity' he did 'seize the venerable pages of Thy Spirit'.[8] Or as it has been put by Rothe in his *Dogmatics*:

> We can speak with good reason of a language of the Holy Spirit. For it lies in the Bible plainly before our eyes, how the Divine Spirit, who is the agent of revelation, has fashioned for himself a quite peculiar dialect out of the speech of that people which forms its theatre.[9]

The illumination of the Spirit

Let us go on now to consider the Holy Spirit in relation to the crisis of illumination. It is by the Spirit alone that the scriptures are savingly and spiritually interpreted. He it is who makes subjectively real to us what is in the written word objectively true for us. In this way the word true for experience becomes actual within experience.

> Illumination thus enables the believer to see that the Bible was produced by inspiration of God, and as such has complete divine authority over his faith and practice.[10]

Here we come to the doctrine of the 'inner witness of the Spirit' of which the great Reformers made so much. The *testimonium Spiritus sancti internum* is, according to Strauss, the Achilles' heel of Protestant theology.[11] Roman Catholics appeal to the teaching office of the church for their interpretation of divine truth. Protestants appeal to scripture as its formal principle, and to the inner testimony of the Spirit as the material principle for the apprehension of saving truth. Calvin stressed the Spirit's inner action in the soul which makes effective in faith the objective word of scripture. Those who are inwardly taught by the Holy Spirit, he affirms, acquiesce implicitly in scripture, and accept it as 'from God'.[12] Indeed, he regards the testimony of the Spirit as superior to reason:

> For as God alone can properly bear witness to his own words, so these words will not obtain full credit in the hearts of men until they are sealed by the inner testimony of the Spirit.[13]

In such a declaration Calvin is but approving the scripture's own declarations about itself.

> Only God himself is a sufficient witness to himself. The word of God finds no acceptance until it is sealed by the inner witness of the Spirit, and the heart finds its rest in Scripture only through this inward teaching.[14]

As 'the book of the Spirit', the scriptures find their true message and meaning only under the illumination of the Spirit. For this 'inner testimony of the Holy Spirit is not an extra guarantee nor a necessary correlate of revelation. It is, on the contrary, the very heart of the revelational process.'[15]

The inner witness of the Spirit does not, however, add anything to scripture as God's revelation. Outside scripture there is no saving word of God. As Mueller states: 'the illuminating witness of the Holy Spirit never takes place apart from God's Word as set forth in the Scriptures.'[16] And again: 'Thus the saving witness of the Holy Spirit never occurs outside of or in opposition to the Scriptures.'[17] It is, then, in and of the Spirit that scripture vindicates itself for what it is – the word of God. 'The work of the Spirit terminates on the divinity of Scripture.'[18] This is in fact its final justification. Even Calvin, whose *Institutes* are almost a Christian apologetic, allows that it is foolish to attempt to prove to infidels that the scriptures are the word of God. It can be known as such only in faith: 'therefore does Scripture suffice to give a saving knowledge of God when its certainty is founded on an inward persuasion of the Holy Spirit.'[19]

James Denney echoes this biblical principle in relation to the Word incarnate when he declares:

The Holy Spirit, bearing witness by and with the Word of the evangelists in our hearts, gives us, independent of any criticism, a full persuasion and assurance of the infallible truth and divine authority of the revelation made in him.

The witness of the Spirit to the believer, he adds, enables him, not only *de facto*, but *de jure*, to take the life of Christ recorded in the gospels as a historical life.[20]

> He it is, the living Author,
>   Wakes to life the sacred word;
> Reads with us its holy pages
>   And reveals our risen Lord.

> *E. Margaret Clarkson*

Or, as Bernard Ramm says,

Only the Holy Spirit can make the printed page the Word of Life; only the Holy Spirit can make the historical Christ a present person; only the Holy Spirit can make theological notions saving truth; only the Holy Spirit can move the mind out of historical probability into divine certainty.[21]

But there is need to insist on the permanent relationship between the Spirit and the word, this despite the tendency of some in every age to divorce what God has joined together. Sometimes emphasis has been on the word to the exclusion of the Spirit; the result has been a cold and lifeless orthodoxy. There is, then, to borrow a line from T. S. Eliot, 'Knowledge of words, and ignorance of the Word.'[22] At other times interest has centred on the Spirit apart from the word, which leads to an individual fanaticism. Here comes the danger of what P. T. Forsyth refers to as 'spiritual vagrancy'.

The Reformers were at one in stressing the relationship between the objective word and the inner witness of the Spirit. Both Calvin and Luther maintained the sovereign right of the Spirit to act as he wills; but they contended that in relation to man's salvation the Spirit never acts apart from the word. Thus Calvin in a comment on Ezekiel 2:2, declares:

The work of the Spirit, then, is joined to the Word of God. But a distinction is made, that we may know that the external Word is of no avail by itself, unless animated by the power of the Spirit.

In the course of time, however, a divorce was contrived between the Spirit and the word. Some began to assert that the word held in itself, as it were mechanically, saving power. This resulted in faith's being regarded more in terms of assent to true doctrine, thus tending to drain the warmth and glow out of Christian commitment. On the other hand, there came together groups of people, characterized by Thomas Watson as those who, 'pretending to have the Spirit, lay aside the whole Bible, and say the Scripture is a dead letter, and they live above it'.[23] I have traced in another volume the fortunes of these two divergent streams,[24] and need not go into further details here.

A right relation between Spirit and word does, however, need statement. It is neither the word apart from the Spirit nor the Spirit apart from the word which is the true biblical position. The scriptures themselves, on their side, give witness to the reality and actuality of the Spirit; they give the assurance that the Spirit has come. And they proclaim further that the Spirit will verify to our understanding the truth of that which the scriptures declare. On the other hand, the Spirit makes authentic the reality of the Christ who has come. But it is through the scriptural revelation we know that he has come, from its pages we learn the certainty of his incarnation and the significance of his cross. Luther viewed the relationship between the Spirit and the scripture as circular. One must have the Spirit in order to understand the scriptures; while it is through the scriptures that the Spirit is given.[25] It is when, as William Cowper puts it in his well-known hymn, the Spirit breathes upon the word, that the truth comes to sight. Then do its precepts and promises afford their sanctifying light.

The doctrinal preacher, it may be, tends to emphasize the word; the eager evangelist may tend to stress the witness of the Spirit. An historical illustration of these two contrasting approaches is that of Charles Simeon and John Wesley. Few will deny that Simeon was a masterly expositor of the scriptures. The twenty-one volumes of his works demonstrate his ability to unfold the meaning of the biblical text. To him the Bible was in all its parts in very truth the word of God; and he took pains to elaborate its meaning. But he was careful to insist on the need of the Spirit's illumination both to interpret and apply the word to the life. Typical is such a statement as this: 'It is by the Scriptures that the Holy Spirit speaks to men.'[26] Or again: 'We are therefore to submit to the teaching of God's word and Spirit.'[27] He can indeed say: 'It is not the word that does good; but the Holy Spirit by the word.'[28]

Wesley, on the other hand, gave prominence to the subjective action of the Holy Spirit. Although he argued strongly for the full inspiration and complete accuracy of the scriptures, he can still declare, 'We know that there is no inherent power in the letter of the Scripture read.'[29] Without the Spirit, he contends, the sacred oracles are a 'dead letter'. But Wesley will not have the Spirit apart from the word. He writes eloquently on 'the witness of the Spirit', but he insists that that witness is by the word. 'God by His word and Spirit, is always with us'[30] – such, we may say, is Wesley's final position. The contrast, then, between Charles Simeon, the evangelical Calvinist, and John Wesley, the evangelical Arminian, may be put like this. For Charles Simeon, revelation is in the word through the Spirit; for John Wesley, revelation is by the Spirit through the word. Whether, therefore, we start from the scripture or the Spirit this relationship must be maintained. For scripture without the Spirit makes for a fruitless faith; while the Spirit without scripture gives an undisciplined faith. The one makes for a dead orthodoxy; the other for an unrestrained enthusiasm. The one gives lifelessness to the church; the other licence to the individual. A scripture without the Spirit is numb; the Spirit without the scripture is nebulous. Put positively in the neat remark of Bernard Ramm, the position of the relationship between the scripture and the Spirit is this: 'The Scriptures function in the ministry of the Spirit, and the Spirit functions in the instrument of the Word.'[31]

In these days there is a preoccupation with the Spirit which may not be of the Spirit, a tendency to conceive of the Spirit acting apart from the word. But always and everywhere the Spirit bears witness to Christ. Christ is the supreme witness of the Spirit. But Christ is, besides, the supreme content of the scriptures. So does the Spirit through whom we have received the scriptures mediate and interpret through them Christ the absolute Word. We cannot, then, appeal to the Spirit apart from the Christ revealed in the scriptures; and there is little sense in appealing to the scriptures apart from the inner witness and understanding illumination of the Spirit. Spirit and word agree. We must affirm that while 'the Holy Spirit can,' he 'does not ordinarily, work without the Word; and that therefore in the work of redemption the Word and the Spirit work together'.[32]

What, then, is basic for Christian faith is a balanced relationship of the perfect form – the objective Word, and the perfect content – the Word applied subjectively in the believing heart by the Holy Spirit. It is 'when God's Spirit joins himself with the chariot of his Word, it becomes effectual'.[33] The words of Abraham Kuyper may be taken as a good summary of the matter of the relationship between the Spirit and the scriptures:

> The witness of this central revelation (of God) which neither repeats nor continues itself, lies for us in the Holy Scriptures. Not, of course as though the Bible by itself were sufficient to give, to everyone who reads it, a true knowledge of God. We positively reject such a mechanical explanation; and by their teaching of the witness of the Holy Spirit as absolutely indispensable for all *conviction* concerning the Scripture, by their requirement of illumination for the *right understanding* of the Scripture, and by their high esteem of the ministry of the Word for the *application* of the Scripture, our fathers have sufficiently shown that such a mechanical explanation cannot be ascribed to them.[34]

The Spirit and evangelism

We can add only a few lines on the Spirit in relation to the proclaimed word. In his discourse in the Upper Room, our Lord himself brought the witness of the word and the witness of the Spirit into the closest association. The Spirit of Truth, who proceeds from the Father, he shall bear witness of me, Jesus declares; and he adds, and you also are witnesses (cf. John 15:26, 27). The apostles were commissioned to proclaim the word concerning Christ, and with it there is the promise of the Holy Spirit as senior partner in the undertaking. So did the word of God, the message of salvation, come in power, and in the Holy Spirit (1 Thessalonians 1:5; cf. Acts 10:44; 2 Corinthians 6:7, etc.). The things which were announced by those who preached the good news, Peter asserts and assures, were through the Holy Spirit sent down from heaven (cf. 1 Peter 1:5). As it is put by Luther, the Father 'sends his Holy Spirit to preach Christ in my heart'.[35]

This is the same gospel of God, the word embodied in the scriptures of truth, which is still to be proclaimed. And it is for those who mix it with faith, God's very own word, authenticated as such by the Spirit in the believing heart. The word preached in the power of the Spirit is a sharp two-edged sword; and in the hands of apostolic men it becomes what it truly is, 'The sword of the Spirit which is the word of God.' (Ephesians 6:17.)

9
INTERPRETING THE BIBLICAL FAITH

The need for belief

The Bible has something to say about its own interpretation. It is to be interpreted *believingly*. The one who would know what the scriptures are all about must be warned at the beginning that he will find their true meaning locked from him unless he approaches them aright. If approached merely as a source book of antiquated beliefs, or, at most, a collection of influential literature, it is not likely that the reader will catch in the words the voice of God. The golden key which unlocks the treasures of the Bible is the acceptance of it as a book that somehow has divine relevance to one's own life and that of the world. The dictum is, then, in Augustine's famous phrase: we must believe that we may know.

We are often told to approach the Bible with an open mind. But an open mind may well mean a prejudiced head and a closed heart. Bultmann tells us that the interpretation of the biblical writings is not subject to conditions different from those applying to other kinds of literature.[1] Such a statement is, in a sense, both true and false. It is true because we are dealing with literature; with what is written. It is false if we regard the Bible as – in every respect – like all other kinds of literature.

The preceding chapters have tried to make it clear that this is not so. Nevertheless there is no set way of approaching every sort of writing; the type of the literature conditions the nature of the approach. We just cannot help coming to a reading of any work without presuppositions. Thus, as Ernst Kinder remarks,

If we do not approach the Bible from the standpoint of the Church, we do so from the standpoint of some world view. There is no third possibility such as neutrality without presuppositions.[2]

Interpreting the Bible can only be done in the sure certainty of its yielding up its message if the purpose of the writings is acknowledged at the outset. It asserts throughout that it has things to say about God: and it carries throughout the marks of its divine inspiration.

Spiritual illumination

Then again, the Bible is to be interpreted *spiritually*. We are aware that this word can be misunderstood – used, as we shall see below, to support a specific methodology. But what we intend is only what the scripture itself says, that spiritual things are spiritually discerned (cf. 1 Corinthians 2:14). For such spiritual discernment there must be the illumination of the Holy Spirit. What was revealed through the Spirit, we are brought to understand by the Spirit; for it is the Spirit who teaches (cf. 1 Corinthians 2:10–14). The Bible is God's book; 'the very Scripture of the Holy Spirit,' to recall Luther's designation of it. Since, then, it is the Holy Spirit who impelled its authors to speak the truth about God's self-disclosure, it follows that 'it is the Holy Spirit who can interpret what he has caused them to speak'.[3] The Holy Spirit – 'the Spirit of truth' – has come in fulfilment of our Lord's promise to be our guide 'into everything that is true' (John 15:13, Phillips).

The centrality of Christ

The Bible, further, is to be interpreted *christologically*. This obviously goes for the New Testament. The gospels tell us of the reality and basis of faith in the life and work of Christ; Acts describes the birth and development of the church in the experience of Christ; the epistles set forth the new life and required style of living in the grace of Christ; and the Revelation points us to the final victory of Christ.

But a christological reading of the Old Testament is no less required, and is stamped with Christ's own approval. He constantly quoted the Old Testament in relation to his own life and work – on the Emmaus highway calmly rebuked the journeying disciples for their failure to do so. Then 'beginning with Moses and all the prophets, he interpreted to them in all the scriptures the things concerning himself' (Luke 24:27). 'To him who believes,' declares F. X. Durwell, 'our Lord's face appears even in the pages of the Old Testament. It is Christ, dead and risen again, who gives the whole Bible its unity and meaning.'[4] It was therefore proper for Irenaeus to say that 'the writings of Moses are the words of Christ.'[5] For 'the words of Christ,' Origen explains, are not 'only those which he spoke when he became man and tabernacled in the flesh, for before that time, Christ, the Logos of God, was in Moses and the prophets.'[6] 'Viewing the Old Testament christologically, is not, as Norman Geisler says, 'an interpretative (hermeneutical) option; for the Christian it is a divine imperative.'[7]

Some recent biblical scholars, reacting from the blatant denial by leaders of other schools of thought, notably that of Bultmann, who see little or no connection between the New Testament and the Old, have strongly advocated the christological canon of Old Testament interpretation. Von Rad, for example, finds everywhere in the history of the Old Testament brought to pass by God's word, whether in acts of judgement or redemption, the prefiguration of the event of Christ in the New Testament.[8] This principle has been carried through in the most radical manner by Barth and his followers. Barth sees both Testaments as mutually witnessing to each other, and thus jointly witnessing to the one Jesus Christ.[9] This was, of course, Luther's great principle. He sought Christ in every part of the Old Testament. 'Take Christ from the Scriptures – and what more will you find in them?' asks Luther rhetorically, to have the answer returned: 'Nothing.'[10]

Yet there is danger when this right and necessary christological principle is elevated into a topological method in which fancy plays a larger part than enlightened understanding. There cannot be some hidden meaning in every detail of the Old Testament. And it would seem to profit nothing to seek for such in, for example, every tassel on the tabernacle's furnishings, every tab on the high priest's garments; and especially so when what is usually found is clearly given elsewhere. Still there are types which have their christological significance, as Jesus himself made clear. He pointed to the uplifted serpent in the wilderness as suggestive of the healing effect of his cross. There are, nevertheless, symbols and ceremonies in the Old Testament with the sole purpose of bringing God's word home effectively to the people of the time. The truth remains, however, that the full sweep of Old Testament history and the utterances of the prophets had a messianic intent.

The first part of the above statement indicates that some place must therefore be given to the historical interpretation of the Old Testament. By using the historical material of the Old Testament to illustrate Christian truth, and to reinforce the ethical requirements of the gospel, the New Testament is thereby not only authenticating the basic historicity of the former word, but is at the same time firmly connecting the Word of God with actual historical events. Instances of this fact are abundant: the story of the Flood; David's eating of the shew-bread; Jonah and the great fish; Elijah's prayer for rain; the patience of Job.

The second part of the statement made above – that the utterances of the prophets have a messianic intent – is confirmed by the many references in the New Testament back to the Old, and the frequency of the formula, 'as it is written', or, 'that it might be fulfilled', throughout the gospels connecting it with Jesus the Messiah. So evident, indeed, is this fact that some scholars suggest that the promise/fulfilment category is the surest way to understand the relation between the two Testaments. In the Old Testament the future of the Messiah is foretold; in the New Testament it finds fulfilment. It may then truly be said:

The *sola scriptura* principle ultimately has meaning only in the unfolding of Scripture's christological content and its soteriological purpose. The *sola scriptura* principle has its validity and authority only from the Holy Scriptures authored by God and used to bring men to faith in Jesus Christ.[11]

The need for openness

The scriptures are to be interpreted *openly*. It is not the case, as some have contended, that the Bible holds some secret word for the spiritually and privately initiated. The famous Alexandrian School of exegetes, notably Clement and Origen, sought by the use of the allegorical method to divine a secret meaning in the biblical text. Clement taught that scripture had a three-fold meaning, and this was compared by Origen, his successor, to the tripartite nature of man. As man is a totality of three elements – body, soul and spirit; so too, he suggested, is scripture. The literal meaning he compares to the body; the moral to the soul; and the spiritual to the spirit. But he could not maintain his tripartite distinction, and ended up with a dualism between the literal and spiritual interpretation. Origen thence repudiated the literal interpretation, but allowed it to be enough for the simple believer and the unenlightened mind. He reserved the allegorical, or spiritual, meaning for such as could not penetrate into the deeper things beyond the letter. But

> the Holy Scripture is no Delphic oracle to bewilder and mislead the human heart by utterances of double meaning. God's written word, taken as a whole, and allowed to speak for itself, will be found its own best interpreter.[12]

This certainly was the Pauline procedure. The apostle would have all believers know the truth in its entirety. He was pleased to say that he proclaimed the gospel fully (Romans 15:19). He did not hold anything back. He always acted on the principle that all believers could grasp the open secret of God's unveiling (cf. Ephesians 3:7f.).

And the scriptures must be interpreted *honestly*. The apostolic preachers were aware that those who preached the word did not always do so with pure motive and good conscience. But it is for all Christians to know the truth and to share with all those 'holding forth the Word of life' (Philippians 2:16, AV). For we do not interpret scripture honestly, merely to secure ourselves in our own entrenched opinions, or to separate us from other believers who do not fully echo our views. We are, therefore bidden to 'use no hocus-pocus, no clever tricks, no dishonest manipulation of the word of God' (2 Corinthians 2:4, Phillips).

Studying the Bible

Then again must we interpret the Bible *dexterously*; and so be 'a workman that needeth not to be ashamed, rightly dividing the word of truth' (2 Timothy 2:15, AV) or, as it is in the NEB, 'a labourer who need not be ashamed driving a straight furrow, in the proclamation of the truth'. The general meaning here is plain, though the actual figure is uncertain.

> The picture may be that of a mason 'squaring' his bricks; a ploughman cutting a straight furrow; or a man making a road straight to his destination. The thought is suggested that in the preaching of Christ in any one given sermon it is not great slabs of truth which should be passed on, rough-hewn from the quarry of the gospel. The preacher should give one brick at a time, rightly proportionated and fitting in easily with the bricks which have already been given. Or he should move confidently over the territory of gospel truth, not turning to the right or to the left from the gospel into vain speculation or myth.[13]

It is worthwhile to state that the scripture must be interpreted *intelligently*. This is not at all to adopt a rationalistic hermeneutical stance which subjects the word of God to mere human reason. That approach results in scepticism by repudiating whatever there is in scripture which fails to commend itself to the mind.

> All endeavours to produce a non-supernatural Gospel have failed, however; the liberal or rationalistic method stands condemned by its own impotence to account for the Scriptures.[14]

Yet the reason redeemed in Christ must be keenly alive if the Bible is to yield its message clearly to us. For what Peter had to say about the letters of his beloved brother Paul, that they contain some things 'hard to understand' (2 Peter 3:16), is equally true of other scriptures. In this connection, John Stott quotes with approval a statement from Charles Simeon: 'For the attainment of divine knowledge, we are directed to combine a dependence on God's Spirit with our own researches. Let us, then, not presume to separate what God has united.'[15] For all that, it may be well to remember the direction of Alan Stibbs: 'not only that the human understanding is at best finite; but also that individual ability to grasp the fulness of the divine truth is still more limited.'[16]

The principles of interpretation

All we have been saying so far may be regarded as pre-suppositions of biblical interpretation. We have still to consider its principles. A large literature on this topic offers many and various helpful canons for the unfolding of the meaning of the biblical word. Rather than merely reproduce them here, I present in my own way a sixfold methodology which may be useful for discovering what the scriptures have to say to us.

The place the passage occupies

The all-embracing principle for the interpretation of scripture is the recognition that its several books constitute a unity. This means that the key to the understanding of scripture is to be found within itself. When applied to a particular passage this canon requires that it be interpreted in the context of the total biblical scheme.

> The principle that Scripture is to interpret itself ... rests ultimately on the biblical unity of authorship, content, and purpose. The fact that the Scriptures were authored by God the Holy Spirit suggests this principle is ultimately an extension of the general hermeneutical principle of literary exegesis that any passage must be considered in terms of its context. Thus the context of any Bible passage is the entire Scripture, since all Scripture is authored by the same Holy Spirit.[17]

There is an over-all harmony in the book of God, and no specific section can, in the last resort, be at odds with God's unfolding disclosure of his purposes for man's salvation. It is, in fact, in this context that a resolution of apparent contradictions between one book and another, one passage and another, must be sought. The whole general meaning of God's word, for example, is that salvation is by grace through faith. Neither the law of the Old Testament dispensation nor the words of the Epistle of James (2:14–26) can be finally out of harmony with this fact. It is sometimes stated that the Old Testament presents the 'law' as a means of salvation for those in pre-New Testament times. Not so. God's dealing with sinful men is always a matter of grace; and the law of the old dispensation was given to a nation which had been redeemed and delivered by God's own mighty acts of grace.

But not only must the passage find its interpretation in harmony with the whole biblical revelation, it must also be related to its immediate context. The meaning of dominant words in a particular section is sometimes modified by the connection in which they are used. Reference to the context will prevent us from taking the Bible as a scrap book of pious religious jottings to be picked out at random. God did not give us the Bible, as has been said, in the form of tear-off calendars with a verse per day. Luther speaks harshly of those who use the Bible in this way, who merely pick out a word, torture it with their figures, and nail it to the cross of their own chosen meaning, and utterly disregard the surrounding context and the author's aim and intention.

The sense the words intend

By this statement we are to understand that the terms before us in the biblical record are to be given their plain, natural meaning. Such was the main canon of biblical interpretation advanced by the Reformers. They repudiated the prevailing allegorical methodology which too often wrested the biblical record in an effort to find justification for some novel churchly doctrine. 'The true meaning of Scripture is the natural and obvious meaning; and let us embrace and abide by it resolutely,' declares Calvin in a comment on Galatians 4:22. Some prefer the term *literal* to that of natural; and are emphatic that the literal, or strictly grammatical, use of terms is the fundamental rule for interpreting the Bible, as indeed it is for any other book.

In the last analysis, our theology finds its solid foundation only in its grammatical sense of Scripture. Theological knowledge will be faulty in proportion to its deviation from the plain meaning of the Bible.[18]

We must distinguish between literalism and letteralism. There is a letteralistic interpretation of scripture which leads to crude results, as when certain levitical prohibitions are taken out of context and forced upon Christian believers. Letteralism is concerned with the letter; it is restricted only to the letter. Literalism, on the other hand, is concerned with truth; it discovers the truth in the letter. But by maintaining a literalistic canon we are not refusing to allow that there are metaphor, simile and parable in the Bible. There obviously are. But this does not mean the abandonment of obedience to the natural or literal sense. It is but to insist that the 'words must still be taken in their grammatical sense, though that sense will vary as the style of the writing departs from prose and conforms to one or another of the modes of figurative speech.'[19] To admit the presence of figurative speech is not to deny literal interpretation.

The main passage on which Origen relied for his allegorical method of interpretation is Galatians 4:24f. But when this passage is examined in the light of its historical context it is clear that the basic literal facts remain. 'Now this is an allegory,' says Paul in verse 24. Paul is not asserting that the Old Testament record itself is a mere allegorical tale. His meaning is that these things are said allegorically, since the story itself has another significance besides the historical one. Yet by an allegory, Paul does not intend a mere illustration. He sees a spiritual truth embodied in the history, 'a shadow from the eternal world cast upon the sands of time'[20]. Therefore when 'it is affirmed that the Bible is literally true, it is not implied that it contains no metaphorical elements, but merely that what is said metaphorically must be understood to be its real meaning'[21].

The method the literary style requires

Having acknowledged that many types of literary form are to be found in the Bible and that the literal interpretation is the right one, the exegete must still have regard to the specific type. He must recognize what is prose, what is poetry, and what is parable. And he will seek the truth of God in each. But he will let the biblical word speak for itself and not impose upon it a meaning it does not intend.

It is wrong, for example, to build a doctrine on some incidental detail of Jesus' parables as we have them in the gospels. In spite of the difficulty occasioned by Mark 4:12, Jesus evidently used the parabolic method to make his teaching clearer and easier to understand. But the golden key is to recognize that in each parable there is a dominant thought which finds its significance in the context of its primary situation and condition. In interpreting parables, therefore, the main point must be grasped and the unessential details not pressed.

The message the section conveys

It is necessary for the interpretation of scripture to put certain questions to the text of which the meaning is being sought. What, for example, does the passage teach about God's ways with man? How was that word understood by those to whom it first came? And how has it meaning for the people of God in the contemporary situation? In answering these questions, the exegete will wish to distinguish between what is of permanent validity and what belongs to a stipulated period. 'It is fatal,' says J. Stafford Wright, 'to assume that every Scripture is of permanent validity irrespective of the circumstances in which it was given. The Levitical prescriptions are an example of this.'[22]

The light clearer references give

There are certainly in the Bible passages obscure and difficult to understand. They remain so, however long pondered over, until light is shed upon them from passages where the meaning is plain. It is in the shining of their own brightness that the scriptures themselves are illuminated. And its specific dark places can be lit up in the excess of light of its own clear rays. Such then is the rule: 'interpret Scripture by Scripture, especially what is obscure by what is plain.'[23] From light to dark should be the movement. Such, according to Richard Marius, was Luther's 'famous idea that the scripture was its own interpreter.' By this simple approach to the Bible was he able 'to declare an independence from ecclesiastical tradition'[24].

A typical obscure passage illustrating this procedure is that of Hebrews 6:4–6. These verses apparently affirm the possibility of apostasy on the part of Christian believers. How is the interpreter to go about bringing out the true teaching of such a passage? He will recognize, to begin with, that the Epistle to the Hebrews is written against an Old Testament background. This will suggest at once that light may be shed upon the author's thought if its specific ideas are considered as they occur in their Old Testament context. Then the sense of the passage must be sought by fuller examination of the New Testament significance of the important terms – repentance, enlightened, heavenly gifts, world to come. The question has then to be asked, does this passage teach emphatically that true believers can fall away and be lost? If answered in the affirmative there has to be considered further, does this conclusion really harmonize with other statements in the context, the declarations, for instance, 'the full assurance of hope until the end', and 'those who inherit the promises'? And what of the wider context of biblical teaching on the issue? If other passages are found to be unequivocal regarding the eternal security of the truly born again, then the passage must be approached again, and its interpretation sought in the light shed from what these other scriptures clearly affirm.

The situation the verses suggest

We have already stated that every passage of scripture must be considered in its proper context. This context, however, includes more than its immediate verbal setting or, indeed, its general harmony with the whole revelation. It has to do also with the historical, geographical and cultural occasion and situation; all have to be taken into account rightly to interpret the biblical message. The self-disclosure of God covered a long period of history, yet each successive era had its own geographical boundaries and its own cultural patterns. Full recognition must be taken of these facts, which means that

we can discern the permanent principles in the biblical document only when we first of all relate that document to the conditions of its own times; we shall then be better able to reapply to our own times those features of its teaching which are valid for all time.[25]

Exposition

The rest of this chapter will be concerned with a plea for serious biblical interpretation, for sound exegesis, for expository preaching. But such can only be as the church constantly affirms faith in the divinity of its scriptures, for it is with this presupposition that the Bible interpreter and expositor approaches his task. Very different is this presupposition from that of those who seek to expound Plato or Aristotle. Unlike other ancient writings, the Bible is not a word from the dead past. It is God's word in the living present. In its pages the gospel of Christ, the good news of God, is made contemporary. Thus does the biblical word confront man in every age with the issues of eternity. The Bible is quite other than an organ of philosophical thought or scientific intelligence. It is the very sacrament of God to the human soul; of the living God to living, yet lost, men.

The popular, topical preaching characteristic of many modern pulpits serves merely to betray a lack of faith in scripture as the reliable word of God. Such lack of faith is the direct result of a century of critical appraisement of the biblical record during which the Bible has been torn apart, separated out, split up to such an extent that the preacher is left with hardly adequate blocks of acceptable material to expound. The Bible has been wrenched out of the hands of the preacher and he is unable to find a certain word of God to proclaim. Some scholars seem to take a special delight in down-grading Scripture. So much so that a recent writer can, with apparent seriousness, give one of his books the question-begging title, *Is 'Holy Scripture' Christian?* And in its pages he can quote with approval a statement of Ernst Käsemann that when it comes to giving the Bible its true valuation it is the decision of the scholar rather than 'the piety of the pious' which must have the last word.[26] But that verdict has been so often so hesitant and unsure that not only the modern pulpit but the pew also has come to believe that the Bible has little relevance for man come of age in the contemporary world.

The ordinary church-goers do, of course, still expect an occasional reference to it from the pulpit. But for themselves it remains something like a holy relic of another age. The position is, in the words of William Cowper, that

Thousands ...
Kiss the book outside, who ne'er look within.

But the church is strong in the gospel only as it rightly regards the biblical function of the preacher in its midst, and the preacher only as he constantly and consciously renews his faith in the sovereignty of God's Word.

It is of first importance that the expositor should constantly bear in mind that not only are the substance and sentiments expressed in Holy Writ of Divine origin, but that its whole contents are verbally inspired.[27]

The preacher is not there to gratify the desire for modernity, for subjectivism, for spurious spirituality. He is there as the interpreter of the word; and is thus the voice of the church. For 'the work of interpretation can be done adequately only within the life of the whole church ... (it) is an expression both of the church's genuine concern for the Bible and the means of commending the gospel.'[28]

It follows, therefore, as P. T. Forsyth has said, that

nothing in the service goes to the root of the gospel (and, therefore, of the church) like preaching. And that makes preaching the chief part of our evangelical ritual, the part which gives the law to all worship, since the message is what stirs worship and makes it possible. Our chief praise is thanksgiving for the gospel. And our prayer is Christian only in the name of the gospel. Preaching is 'the organized Hallelujah of an ordered community'.[29]

The interpreter of the word has his calling from God. From the church he receives at most his licence, his opportunity. The church may supply the pulpit; God must confer the authority. From the church the preacher may have his permission; but from God he has commission. The preacher, so ordained of God, is truly an officer of the word; an expositor of God's revelation; a man of the book. As long as he remains faithful to that calling he may be confident that the Lord who gave the book will bless the book.

All this means that to interpret scripture is a more exacting thing than getting a thought for today; good exposition only comes after serious exploration. The one who would open up the word must dig deep if he would find the treasure hid in the field. In order to be a faithful interpreter, every theologian must be adept at weighing different interpretations, using his expertise as a grammarian to be a true witness. The expositor of the word will ask questions of the passage he would expound, questions such as, 'What does it teach about God's way for man?' but he will

> keep in mind as a general principle that this literature is unique in that it conveys to men God's Word in Christ; it makes possible a knowledge of Christ which means actual contact with the redemptive action of God. Each passage should be related to that central affirmation, and the expositor's aim is so to set it forth that the Jesus of history becomes the Christ of faith; in other words, that the original Jesus does not remain the Man of Galilee, but emerges as the contemporary Master of the believer today.[30]

The expositor of scripture is essentially the servant of the word for the sake of God's church and God's world. But the servant of the word for the church first; since duty to the world is the joint requirement of both preacher and church. It is the calling of the minister of the word to translate to his small church the word entrusted to the great church. Thus does the minister of the local church confirm his apostolic succession in the word commissioned to the whole church. For the great apostolate is one, not first, and maybe not at all, in the heredity of an historic line, but rather in the solidarity of the historic gospel; not certainly in a continuous stream, but absolutely in a divine scripture.

Honest interpretation of the Bible demands some corresponding experience. To be sure, no preacher can make his experience the measure of his preaching. That would make it too thin, too meagre. And besides, there is more in God's revelation than any one can ever experience or, indeed, ever explore. At the same time it must be 'the aim of every faithful interpreter to be involved in what he communicates without expanding or contradicting the biblical ideas which he is communicating.'[31] The expositor of the word who would truly communicate the word must live by the word; he must in his measure incarnate in himself its holy message. C. H. Spurgeon declares that Bunyan's very blood was 'biblized'. He stood before the people with his Bible in his hand because he had first taken it to his heart. Thus for the interpreter of the Bible Bengel's dictum stands: 'First apply yourself to the text, and then apply the whole to yourself.' In this way the ideal ministry will then be what Forsyth calls a 'bibliocrasy'. For the true expositor speaks from within the sanctuary of God's word.

NOTES

Chapter One

1 Emil Brunner, *Revelation and Reason*, trans. Olive Wyon, London, SCM Press 1947, page 44.
2 Søren Kierkegaard, *Attack on 'Christendom', 1854–1855*, trans. Walter Lowrie, Oxford University Press, London 1946, page 32.
3 F. Gerald Dowling, *Has Christianity a Revelation?*, London, SCM Press 1964.
4 H. D. McDonald, 'Revelation', *The New International Dictionary of the Christian Church*, ed. J. D. Douglas, Grand Rapids, Zondervan 1974, page 843.
5 Leon Morris, *I Believe in Revelation*, Grand Rapids, Eerdmans 1976, page 19.
6 Cf. Dewey M. Beegle, *Scripture, Tradition and Infallibility*, Grand Rapids, Eerdmans 1973, pages 25f.
7 H. R. Mackintosh, *The Christian Apprehension of God*, London, SCM Press 1929, pages 64f.
8 H. H. Farmer, *The World and God*, London, Nisbet 1935, page 79.
9 J. A. Motyer, 'Name', *The New Bible Dictionary*, ed. J. D. Douglas, London, Inter-Varsity Press 1962, page 863.
10 Louis Berkhof, *Systematic Theology*, London, Banner of Truth 1958, page 47.
11 H. Bavinck, *The Doctrine of God*, Grand Rapids, Eerdmans 1951, page 130.
12 *Ibid.*
13 *Ibid.*
14 Carl F. H. Henry, *God, Revelation, and Authority*, Waco, Texas, Word 1976, vol. 2, page 181.
15 Emil Brunner, *The Mediator: A Study in the Central Doctrine of the Christian Faith*, trans. Olive Wyon, London, Lutterworth Press 1934, page 21.
16 Henry, *op. cit.*, page 8; cf. pages 17f.
17 H. P. Owen, *The Knowledge of God*, London, Athlone Press 1969, page 43.
18 Henry, *op. cit.*, pages 85, 86.
19 John Calvin, *The Institutes of the Christian Religion*, Beveridge's Translation, London, James Clark 1949, page 51.
20 Brunner, *op. cit.*, pages 72, 73.
21 Helmut Thielicke, *How the World Began: Sermons on the Creation Story*, Cambridge and London, James Clarke 1964, page 49.

22 H. Wheeler Robinson, *Inspiration and Revelation in the Old Testament*, New York, Oxford University Press 1946, page 4.
23 Cf. B. B. Warfield, *The Inspiration and Authority of the Bible*, ed. Samuel A. Craig, Philadelphia, The Presbyterian and Reformed Publishing Company 1970, pages 96f.
24 Henry, *op. cit.*, page 82.
25 E. Y. Mullins, *Freedom and Authority in Religion*, Philadelphia, The Griffith and Rowland Press 1913, page 315.
26 Thomas F. Torrance, *Space, Time and Incarnation*, London, Oxford University Press 1969, page 24.

Chapter Two
1 H. Bavinck, *The Philosophy of Religion*, Grand Rapids, Eerdmans 1953, page 20.
2 B. Ramm, *Special Revelation and the Word of God*, Grand Rapids, Eerdmans 1961, page 19.
3 Emil Brunner, *Revelation and Reason*, page 47.
4 Carl F. H. Henry, *God, Revelation and Authority*, vol. 2, page 56.
5 *Ibid.*, page 11; cf. pages 247ff.
6 P. K. Jewett, 'Special Revelation as Historical and Personal' *Revelation and the Bible*, ed. Carl F. H. Henry, London, Tyndale Press 1959, page 46.
7 Norman H. Snaith, *The Distinctive Ideas of the Old Testament*, London, Epworth Press 1944, page 139.
8 Cf. Leon Morris, *I Believe in Revelation*, Grand Rapids, Eerdmans.
9 *Ibid.*, page 111.
10 Alan Richardson, *Christian Apologetics*, London, SCM Press, page 145.
11 Cf. W. Temple, *Nature, Man and God*, London, Macmillan 1951, pages 301–327.
12 Hugo Meynell, *Journal of Theological Studies*, new series, Vol. XXIV, 1973, page 157.
13 H. H. Rowley, *The Faith of Israel*, London, SCM Press 1956, Intro. page 21.
14 Donald Mackinnon, *Borderlands of Theology*, London, Lutterworth Press 1968, page 82.
15 H. D. McDonald, *Ideas of Revelation: 1700–1860*, London, Macmillan 1959, page 272.
16 Rene Pache, *The Inspiration and Authority of Scripture*, trans. Helen I. Needham, Chicago, Moody Press 1969, page 32.
17 John Calvin, *Institutes* 1, page 68.
18 P. T. Forsyth, *The Person and Place of Jesus Christ*, London, Independent Press, new edition 1946, page 171.
19 James Orr, *Revelation and Inspiration*, London, Duckworth 1910, page 155.
20 Morris, *op. cit.*, page 118.
21 W. J. Martin, 'Special Revelation as Objective', *Revelation and the Bible*, 1958, pages 63f.
22 Clark H. Pinnock, *Biblical Revelation*, Chicago, Moody Press 1971, page 35.
23 N. B. Stonehouse, 'Special Revelation as Scriptural', *Revelation and the Bible*, page 81.
24 James D. Smart, *The Strange Silence of the Bible in the Church*, London, SCM Press 1970, page 98.

25 Brunner, *op. cit.*, page 7.
26 Cf. C. H. Dodd, *The Authority of the Bible*, London, Nisbet 1928, pages 24ff.
27 Brunner, *op. cit.*, pages 7, 21.

Chapter Three

1 Hans Küng, *On Being a Christian*, trans. Edward Quinn, London, Collins 1977, page 466.
2 James Orr, *Revelation and Inspiration*, page 159.
3 Report of Committee 1, Chairman, A. M. Ramsey, Archbishop of York, *The Holy Bible: Its Authority and Message*, London, SPCK 1959, page 21.
4 Peter Brown, *Augustine of Hippo*, London, Faber & Faber 1968, page 252.
5 John Calvin, *Institutes* 1, chapter vi, 3, page 66.
6 Heindrick Bornhamm, *Luther's World of Thought*, trans. Martin H. Bertram, St. Louis, Concordia 1965, page 72.
7 G. P. Fisher, *History of Christian Doctrine*, Edinburgh, T. & T. Clark 1902, page 280; cf. Julius Kostlin, *The Theology of Luther*, trans. Charles E. Gray, Philadelphia, Lutheran Publication Society 1897, page 252. W. P. Patterson, *The Rule of Faith*, London, Hodder and Stoughton 1912, page 405. M. Reu, *Luther and the Scriptures*, Columbus, Ohio, Warburg Press 1944, pages 17, 24, 63, 92, etc.
8 Martin Luther, *Epistle Sermon, Second Sunday in Advent*, Luther's Works vol. vii, 34, Lenker edition, quoted in Hugh Thompson Kerr, *A Compound of Luther's Theology*, London, SCM Press 1943, page 10.
9 Quoted in Gerhard Ebeling, *The Word of God and Tradition*, trans. S. H. Hooke, London, Collins 1968, page 175.
10 Thomas Watson, *The Body of Divinity*, London, Banner of Truth 1958, pages 18f.
11 Charles Simeon, *Horae Homileticae*, London, Henry C. Bolm, 3rd ed. 1838, vol. 17, page 497.
12 *The Works of John Wesley*, printed at the Conference Centre Office, City Road, London 1809, ed. Joseph Benson, 21 vols. 'On Laying the Foundation Stone of the New Chapel, Ap. 21, 1777'; liv, ii, sect. 2, vol. 8, page 399; 'The Mystery of Iniquity', lxvi, sect. 31, vol. 9, page 217; 'The Signs of the Times', lxxi, ii, sect. 10, vol. 9, page 275; 'On Obedience to Pastors', cii, ii, sect. 7, vol. 10, page 234.
13 *The Works of John Wesley*, 'On Dissipation', lxxxiv, sect. 16, vol. 10, page 7; 'A Clear and Concise Demonstration of the Divine Inspiration', vol. 15, pages 351f. cf. 'A Further Appeal', 6, sect. 1, vol. 12, page 122.
14 Quoted in Bernard Ramm, *Special Revelation and the Word of God*, Grand Rapids, Eerdmans 1961, page 81.
15 John MacLeod, *Scottish Theology: Lectures Delivered at Westminster Theological Seminary, USA*, Edinburgh, Free Church Publication Committee 1943, pages 313, 314.
16 J. W. C. Wand, *The Authority of the Scriptures*, London, Religious Book Club 1950, page 87.
17 Gabriel Morgan, *The Theology of Revelation*, London, Burns & Oates 1967, page 98.
18 Gabriel Morgan, *op. cit.*, page 97.

19 J. K. Mozley, *The Christian Faith: Essays in Explanation and Defence*, ed. W. R. Matthews, London, Eyre and Spottiswoode 1936, page 55.
20 F. W. Farrar, *The Bible, Its Meaning and Supremacy*, London 1897, page 136.
21 F. W. Farrar, *op. cit.*, page 131.
22 A. S. Peake, *The Bible, Its Origin, Its Significance, and its Abiding Worth*, London, Hodder & Stoughton 1914, pages 398, 399.
23 James Packer, *'Fundamentalism' and the Word of God*, London, Inter-Varsity Fellowship 1958, page 88.
24 L. S. Thornton, *Revelation and the Modern World*, London, Dacre Press 1950, page 130.
25 James Denney, 'The Authority of Christ', *Hastings' Dictionary of the Bible*, ed. J. Hastings, Edinburgh, T. & T. Clark 1906, ad loc.
26 Hans Küng, *op. cit.*, page 477.
27 Emil Brunner, *Reason and Revelation*, page 129.
28 Emil Brunner, *The Philosophy of Religion*, trans. A. J. D. Farrer and Bertram Lee Woolf, London, Ivor Nicholson and Watson 1937, page 153.
29 Emil Brunner, *Our Faith*, trans. John W. Rilling, London, Scribners 1936, page 10.
30 C. H. Dodd, *The Authority of the Bible*, London, Nisbet 1928, page 16.
31 *Ibid.*, page 296.
32 *Ibid.*, page 298.
33 James Barr, *The Bible in the Modern World*, London, SCM Press 1973, page 120.
34 F. F. Bruce, *The Book and the Parchments*, London, Pickering & Inglis 1950, page 15 (italics in text).
35 Jürgen Moltmann, *The Crucified God*, trans. R. A. Wilson and John Bowden, London, SCM Press 1974, pages 66, 67 (italics in text).

Chapter Four
1 James Orr, *Revelation and Inspiration*, page 159 (italics in text).
2 Clark H. Pinnock, *Biblical Revelation*, Chicago, Moody Press 1971, page 53.
3 Clement, *Stromata*, 6, 18, 168, 3.
4 Cf. Gerhart Kittel (ed.), *Theological Dictionary of the New Testament*, trans. and ed. Geoffrey W. Bromiley, Grand Rapids, Eerdmans 1964, page 754.
5 James Orr, *op. cit.*, page 160.
6 Gabriel Morgan, *The Theology of Revelation*, page 112.
7 J. W. Wenham, *Christ and the Scriptures*, London, Tyndale Press 1972, page 9.
8 James D. Smart, *The Interpretation of the Scriptures*, Philadelphia, Westminster Press 1961, pages 184, 185.
9 Clark H. Pinnock, *op. cit.*, page 58.
10 Karl Rahner, *Inspiration in the Scriptures*, New York, Herder & Herder 1961, page 64.
11 G. C. Berkouwer, *Studies in Dogmatics, Holy Scripture*, trans. J. B. Rogers, Grand Rapids, Eerdmans 1975, page 57.
12 Clark H. Pinnock, *op. cit.*, page 57.
13 J. W. C. Wand, *The Authority of the Bible*, page 53.
14 G. C. Berkouwer, *op. cit.*, page 149.

NOTES 151

15 Cf. A. A. Hodge and B. B. Warfield, 'Inspiration', *The Presbyterian Review*, no. 6, Ap. 1881, pages 232f.
16 James D. Smart, *op. cit.*, page 196.
17 J. W. Wenham, *op. cit.*, page 27.
18 H. H. Rowley, *The Relevance of the Bible*, London, James Clarke, 1942, pages 73f. Cf. H. H. Rowley, 'The Inspiration of the Old Testament', *Congregational Quarterly*, vol. 18, April 1940, pages 164–77.
19 G. C. Berkouwer, *op. cit.*, page 158.
20 G. C. Berkouwer, *op. cit.*, pages 158, 159.
21 J. W. C. Wand, *op. cit.*, page 54.
22 James Orr, *op. cit.*, page 209.
23 Karl Rahner, *op. cit.*, pages 14, 15.
24 B. F. Westcott, *Introduction to the Study of the Gospels*, London, Macmillan 1882, page 36.

Chapter Five
1 Austin Farrar, *Saving Belief*, London, Hodder & Stoughton 1964, page 30.
2 E. J. Young, *Thy Word is Truth*, Grand Rapids, Eerdmans 1957, page 113.
3 Alan Richardson, *A Preface to Bible Study*, Philadelphia, Westminster Press 1944, page 33.
4 *Ibid.*
5 J. Burnaby, *Is the Bible Inspired?* (Colet Series of Modern Christian Thought), ed. W. R. Matthews, 1940, pages 112, 113.
6 Marcus M. Dods, *The Bible, Its Origin and Meaning*, London, Scribners 1905, pages 138, 139.
7 Cf. S. R. Driver and A. F. Kirkpatrick, *The Higher Criticism*, London, pages 53f.
8 Charles Gore, *The Doctrine of an Infallible Book*, London, SCM Press 1924, page 7.
9 H. H. Rowley, *The Unity of the Bible*, London 1953, page 15.
10 H. H. Rowley, *The Relevance of the Bible*, London, James Clarke 1942, page 73.
11 H. H. Rowley, *op. cit.*, page 25.
12 *Op. cit.*, page 43.
13 Leon Morris, *I Believe in Revelation*, page 100.
14 *Ibid.*, page 107.
15 A. J. Gordon, *The Ministry of the Spirit*, London, Kingsgate Press, page 182.
16 J. C. Ryle, *The Christian Leaders of the Last Century*, T. Nelson & Sons 1873, page 26.
17 Augustine, *Epistolae*, 82, i, 3.
18 Clark H. Pinnock, *Biblical Revelation*, page 73.
19 James Packer, *'Fundamentalism' and the Word of God*, page 72.
20 Cf. A. G. Hebert, *Fundamentalism and the Church of God*, London 1957, ch. 1.
21 A. G. Hebert, *The Authority of the Old Testament*, London, Faber & Faber 1947, pages 93–100.
22 *Ibid.*, page 22.
23 *Ibid.*, page 98.
24 *Ibid.*, page 307.

25 A. G. Hebert, *Fundamentalism and the Church of God*, pages 55, 56.
26 *Ibid.*, page 47.
27 *Ibid.*, page 55.
28 Leon Morris, *op. cit.*, pages 12, 139.
29 Carl F. H. Henry, 'Inspiration', *Baker's Dictionary of Theology*, Grand Rapids, Baker Book House 1960, page 289
30 Geoffrey W. Bromiley, in *The New Bible Commentary*, ed. F. Davidson, A.M. Stibbs, and E. F. Kevan, London, Inter-Varsity Fellowship 1954, page 22.
31 Cf. James Packer, *op. cit.*, page 95.
32 *Ibid.*
33 Clark H. Pinnock, 'The Inspiration of the New Testament', *The Living Word of Revelation*, ed. Merrill, C. Tenney, Grand Rapids, Zondervan 1968, page 152.
34 James Warwick Montgomery, 'Whither Biblical Inerrancy?', *Christianity Today*, vol. xxi, no. 20, July 29 1977, page 40.
35 Emil Brunner, *Revelation and Reason*, pages 274, 275.
36 R. A. Finlayson, 'Contemporary Ideas of Revelation', *Revelation and the Bible*, page 231.
37 E. J. Young, *op. cit.*, page 136.
38 E. J. Young, *op. cit.*, page 161.
39 *Ibid.*
40 B. B. Warfield, *op. cit.*, page 435.
41 Leon Morris, *The Churchman*, 81:1, Spring 1967, page 27.
42 Joseph Parker, *None Like It*, London, Nisbet 1893, page 73.

Chapter Six

1 R. V. G. Tasker, *The Old Testament in the New Testament*, Grand Rapids, Eerdmans 1963, page 23.
2 *Op. cit.*, page 18.
3 Maisie Spens, *Concerning Himself*, London, Hodder & Stoughton 1945, page 6.
4 Cf. J. W. Wenham, *Christ and the Bible*, London, Tyndale Press 1972, page 27.
5 R. V. G. Tasker, *op. cit.*, page 38.
6 James D. Smart, *The Interpretation of Scripture*, Philadelphia, Westminster Press 1961, page 187.
7 Claus Westermann *The Old Testament and Jesus Christ*, trans. Omar Kaste, Minneapolis, Augsburg Publishing House, 1968, page 13.
8 S. R. Driver, *Introduction to the Literature of the Old Testament*, New York, Scribner's Sons (second edition), 1892, Preface page xiv.
9 J. W. Wenham, *op. cit.*, page 21.
10 R. T. Ottley, *The Doctrine of the Incarnation*, London, Methuen (fourth edition, revised) 1908, page 625.
11 R. T. Ottley, *op. cit.*, page 626.
12 Basil F. C. Atkinson, *The Christian Use of the Old Testament*, London and Toronto, Inter-Varsity Fellowship 1952, pages 13, 14.
13 R. V. G. Tasker, *op. cit.*, page 37.
14 Pierre C. Marcel, 'Our Lord's Use of Scripture', *Revelation and the Bible*, page 133.

15 T. C. Hammond, 'The Fiat of Authority', *Evangelicalism, Essays by Members of the Fellowship of the Evangelical Churchmen*, ed. J. Russell Howden 1925, pages 185, 186.

16 H. C. G. Moule, *Outlines of Christian Doctrine*, London, Hodder & Stoughton 1905, page 5.

17 James Orr, *The Bible Under Trial*, London, Marshall Brothers Ltd (second edition) 1902, page 307.

18 J. W. Wenham, *op. cit.*, page 108.

19 R. T. France, *Jesus and the Old Testament*, London, Inter-Varsity Press 1971, page 224.

20 Claus Westermann, *op. cit.*, page 10.

21 Cf. Henry M. Shire, *Finding the Old Testament in the New*, Philadelphia, Westminster Press 1974, pages 65–72.

22 Henry M. Shire, *op. cit.*, page 56.

23 E. Earle Ellis, *Paul's Use of the Old Testament*, Grand Rapids, Eerdmans 1957, page 115.

24 E. Earle Ellis, *op. cit.*, page 86.

25 Adolf Harnack, *The Origin of the New Testament*, 1914 (Eng. trans. 1925), page 49 (footnote).

26 H. P. Owen, *The Knowledge of God*, London, Athlone Press 1969, page 51.

27 F. X. Durrwell, *Theologians Today: A Series Selected and Edited by Martin Redfern*, London and New York, Sheen & Ward 1972, page 62.

28 H. Martensen, *Christian Dogmatics*, Edinburgh, T. & T. Clark 1898, page 25.

29 D. G. Guthrie, 'Bible' in *Pictorial Dictionary of the Bible*, ed. Merrill C. Tenney, Grand Rapids, Zondervan 1975, vol. 1, page 561.

30 Claus Westermann, *op. cit.*, page 9.

31 Thomas Watson, *The Body of Divinity*, London, The Banner of Truth 1958, page 18.

32 W. H. Griffith-Thomas, *The Principles of Theology*, London, Church House Book Press 1963, pages 125, 126.

33 George Salmon, *The Infallibility of the Church*, London, John Murray 1888; reissue, Grand Rapids, Baker 1959, page 117.

34 P. T. Forsyth, *The Person and Place of Jesus Christ*, London, Independent Press, fifth edition, 1946, page 140. Cf. P. T. Forsyth, *The Principle of Authority*, London, Independent Press, second edition, 1952, pages 96, 142, 146–55.

Chapter Seven

1 John MacLeod, *Scottish Theology*, page 312.

2 D. Martyn Lloyd-Jones, *Authority*, London, Inter-Varsity Fellowship 1958, page 50.

3 P. T. Forsyth, *The Principle of Authority*, page 146.

4 William Temple, *Nature, Man and God*, London, Macmillan 1934, page 20.

5 William Temple, *op. cit.*, pages 348f.

6 Cf. H. H. Farmer, *The World and God*, London, Nisbet 1935, pages 23f., 43f.

7 Donald G. Miller, *The Authority of the Bible*, Grand Rapids, Eerdmans 1972, page 18.

8 P. T. Forsyth, *op. cit.*, page 229.
9 B. B. Warfield, *Inspiration and Authority of the Bible*, page 100.
10 D. Martyn Lloyd-Jones, *op. cit.*, page 15.
11 William Barclay, *By What Authority?* London, Darton, Longman and Todd 1974, page 98.
12 Saphir Philip Athyal, 'The Uniqueness and Authority of Christ', *The New Face of Evangelicalism: An International Symposium on the Lausanne Covenant*, ed. René Padilla, Inter-Varsity Press, Chicago 1976, page 64.
13 Saphir Philip Athyal, *op. cit.*, page 66.
14 William Barclay, *Through the Year with William Barclay*, ed. Denis Duncan, London, Hodder & Stoughton 1972, page 209.
15 Cf. P. T. Forsyth, *The Person and Place of Jesus Christ*, London, Independent Press (fifth edition), 1946, page 151.
16 A. Taylor Innes, *John Knox*, Edinburgh and London, Oliphant, Anderson and Ferrier 1896, page 36.
17 Bernard Ramm, 'Is "Scripture Alone" the Essence of Christianity?' *Biblical Authority*, ed. Jack Rogers, Waco, Texas, Word 1977, page 116.
18 Bernard Ramm, *op. cit.*, page 114.
19 Jürgen Moltmann, *The Crucified God*, trans. R. A. Wilson and John Bowden, London, SCM Press 1947, page 5.
20 Helmut Thielicke, *How the World Began: Sermons on the Creation Story*, page 275.
21 Robert H. Bryant, *The Bible's Authority Today*, Minneapolis, Augsburg Publishing House 1968, page 24; cf. Robert Preus, *The Inspiration of the Scripture*, London, Oliver & Boyd 1955, pages 207f.
22 Thomas Watson, *The Body of Divinity*, page 19.
23 Bernard Ramm, *The Pattern of Authority*, page 41.
24 Herbert Cunliffe-Jones, *The Authority of Biblical Revelation*, Boston, The Pilgrim Press 1948, page 19.

Chapter Eight

1 Herman Schultz, *Old Testament Theology*, trans. J. A. Paterson, Edinburgh, T. & T. Clark 1892, vol. 2, page 184.
2 Thomas Rees, *The Holy Spirit in Thought and Experience*, London, Duckworth 1913, page 12.
3 J. Theodore Mueller, 'The Holy Spirit and the Scriptures', *Revelation and the Bible*, ed. Carl C. F. Henry, pages 267, 268.
4 *Ibid.*, page 269.
5 A. J. Gordon, *The Ministry of the Spirit*, London, Kingsgate Press 1894, page 173.
6 *Ibid.*
7 Cf. Martin Luther's Works in 55 volumes, ed. Jaroslav Pelikan and Helmut T. Lehmann, St Louis, Concordia, and Philadelphia, Fortress Press; vol. 6, page 547; vol. 7, page 638; vol. 47, page 133.
8 *The Confessions of St Augustine, A New Translation*, anon, Oxford and London, Rivingtons 1878, bk. 7, ch. 21, page 189.
9 Rothe, *Dogmatics*, page 238, quoted by A. J. Gordon, *op. cit.*, page 178.
10 Kenneth S. Kantzer, 'The Communication of Revelation', *The Bible: the Living Word of Revelation*, ed. Merrill C. Tenney, Grand Rapids, Eerdmans 1968, page 28.

11 Cf. G. C. Berkouwer, *Studies in Dogmatics, Holy Scripture*, Grand Rapids, Eerdmans 1966, page 40.
12 John Calvin, *Institutes of the Christian Religion*, bk. vii, 5, page 72.
13 *Ibid.*, bk. vii, 4, page 72.
14 G. C. Berkouwer, *op. cit.*, page 41.
15 Gabriel Morgan, *The Philosophy of Revelation*, London, Burns and Oates 1967, page 79.
16 J. Theodore Mueller, *op. cit.*, page 269.
17 *Ibid.*, page 270.
18 Bernard Ramm, *The Witness of the Spirit*, Grand Rapids, Eerdmans 1959, page 107.
19 John Calvin, *op. cit.*, bk. vii, 13, page 83.
20 James Denney, *Studies in Theology*, London, Hodder & Stoughton 1895, page 207.
21 Bernard Ramm, *op. cit.*, page 96.
22 T. S. Eliot, 'Chorus from "The Rock", 1934', *The Complete Poems and Plays of T. S. Eliot*, London, Faber & Faber 1969, page 147.
23 Thomas Watson, *The Body of Divinity*, page 23.
24 Cf. *Theories of Revelation*, London, George Allen & Unwin 1963, page 196.
25 Cf. Editor's Preface, *Martin Luther's Epistle to the Galatians*, London, James Clarke 1953, pages 1–15.
26 Charles Simeon, *Horae Homileticae*, vol. 21, page 499.
27 vol. 20, page 38.
28 vol. 10, pages 284, 285.
29 John Wesley, *The Means of Grace*, xvi, sect. 3, vol. 7, page 255.
30 John Wesley, *The Law Established through Faith*, xxxvii, sect. 6, vol. 8, page 161.
31 Bernard Ramm, *The Pattern of Authority*, Grand Rapids, Eerdmans 1957, page 29.
32 Louis Berkhof, *Systematic Theology*, London, Banner of Truth 1939, page 611.
33 Thomas Watson, *op. cit.*, page 25.
34 Abraham Kuyper, *Principles of Sacred Theology*, trans. Hendrick de Vries, Grand Rapids, Eerdmans 1954, page 360 (italics in text).
35 Martin Luther's Works (see above), vol. 24, page 292.

Chapter Nine

1 Rudolf Bultmann, 'The Problem of Hermeneutics', *Essays*, trans. James C. G. Grieg, London, SCM Press 1955, page 256.
2 Ernst Kinder, 'Historical Criticism and Demythologizing', *Kerygma and Myth*, ed. and trans. Carl E. Braaten and Roy A. Harrisville, New York, Abingdon Press 1962, pages 66, 67.
3 John R. W. Stott, *Understanding the Bible*, London, Scripture Union Paperback 1972, page 207.
4 F. X. Durwell, *Theologians Today*: A series selected and edited by Martin Redfern, New York and London, Sheen and Ward 1975, pages 75, 76.
5 *Haer.*, 4, 2, 3.
6 On First Principles, 1.
7 N. L. Grisler, *Christ: The Key to the Interpretation of the Bible*, Chicago, Moody Press 1968, page 31.

8 Cf. G. von Rad, 'Typological Interpretation of the Old Testament', *Essays on Old Testament Hermeneutics*, pages 25f.

9 Karl Barth, *Church Dogmatics*, i, 2, trans. G. T. Thomson, Edinburgh, T. & T. Clark 1936, page 103.

10 Martin Luther, *The Bondage of the Will*, trans. J. I. Packer and O. R. Johnson, Westwood N.J., Fleming H. Revell Company 1957, page 71.

11 Ralph A. Bohlmann, *Principles of Biblical Interpretation in the Lutheran Tradition*, St Louis, Concordia 1968, page 138.

12 Milton S. Terry, *Biblical Hermeneutics*, Grand Rapids, Zondervan 1961, page 162.

13 Ronald A. Ward, *Commentary on 1 and 2 Timothy and Titus*, Waco, Texas, Word 1974, page 173.

14 E. F. Kevan, 'The Principles of Interpretation', *Revelation and the Bible*, page 191.

15 *Ibid.*, page 213.

16 Alan M. Stibbs, *Understanding God's Word*, London, Inter-Varsity Fellowship 1962, page 38.

17 Ralph A. Bohlmann, *op. cit.*, page 108.

18 Louis Berkhof, *Principles of Biblical Interpretation*, Grand Rapids, Baker 1950, page 74.

19 E. F. Kevan, *op. cit.*, page 294.

20 Cf. H. D. McDonald, *Freedom in Faith: An Exposition of Paul's Epistle to the Galatians*, Glasgow, Pickering and Inglis; Old Tappan, N.J., Revell; 1973, *ad loc.*

21 E. F. Kevan, *op. cit.*, page 294.

22 Page 298.

23 John R. W. Stott, *op. cit.*, page 231.

24 Richard Marius, *Luther*, London, Quartet Books 1975, pages 186, 187.

25 F. F. Bruce, 'Inspiration', *New Bible Dictionary*, ed. J. D. Douglas, London, Inter-Varsity Fellowship 1962, page 567.

26 Christopher Evans, London, SCM Press 1971, page 38. (Evans does, however, allow his question to be 'perhaps foolish', page 36.)

27 A. W. Pink, *Interpretation of the Scriptures*, Grand Rapids, Baker 1972, page 61.

28 James D. Wood, *The Interpretation of the Bible*, London, Duckworth 1958, page 175.

29 P. T. Forsyth, *Positive Preaching and Modern Mind*, London, Hodder & Stoughton 1919, page 95.

30 E. C. Blackman, *Biblical Interpretation*, London, Independent Press 1957, page 202.

31 A. Berkeley Mickelsen, *Interpreting the Bible*, Grand Rapids, Eerdmans 1963, page 57.

INDEX